THE MORAL POINT OF VIEW
A Rational Basis of Ethics

Studies
in Philosophy

Consulting Editor:

V. C. CHAPPELL
The University of Chicago

THE MORAL
POINT OF VIEW

A Rational Basis of Ethics

·

by **KURT BAIER**

University of Pittsburgh

ABRIDGED EDITION WITH A NEW PREFACE

BY THE AUTHOR

Random House · New York

Preface to the Abridged Edition

In preparing this book for the present paperback edition, I have followed one overriding principle: to eliminate everything that is not strictly relevant to my main theme and to rewrite and expand whatever seemed obscure, ambiguous, or downright mistaken. The resulting loss in bulk—though of course painful to me—should by present aesthetic standards be judged an improvement in shape and therefore in allure. To those who like the bare bones covered with more connective tissue than is possible in such a slim volume, I offer this new preface which rounds out gaps and adds a point or two for better grasp. (Those not widely read in moral philosophy might, however, most profitably read it after rather than before the main part of the book.)

My main theme is that moralities are best understood as special forms of social control and as special forms of practical reasoning. Any form of social direction and control must attempt to accomplish two major tasks: to provide for the members of the group an easy way of answering the question of what is required of them by this particular form of direction and control, and to ensure compliance with these requirements. The first task is accomplished by the formulation of appropriate principles, precepts, rules, and regulations in a way which makes them easy to remember, to pass on to others, and to apply in a variety of different circumstances, and by the instruction of the members in these principles, etc. The second task is accomplished by group practices designed to exert pressure on individuals to satisfy these requirements, such as the practice of "investigating" individuals to see whether they have adhered to the appropriate principles, precepts, rules, and regulations, and of "meting out" to them whatever is thought appropriate in the light of these investigations.

Clearly, from the very nature of these two tasks, there must arise a certain inner tension between them. For whereas the proper accomplishment of the first requires a critical attitude towards the received solutions, the opposite seems necessary if the second task is to be accomplished. Those preoccupied with the second task will therefore tend to interfere with those engaged in the first, whereas these latter will be torn between their desire not to undermine the group's unquestioning acceptance of the received principles and precepts, and the desire to point out flaws in them.

The concepts of right and wrong are primarily employed in connection with the first task, the concepts of virtue, guilt, responsibility, and punishment primarily in connection with the second, while the concepts of duty, obligation, moral desert, and justice face both ways.

From the philosophical point of view, the first set of concepts is clearly the most fundamental. The accepted answers to the question of what is right and wrong determine what are a group's moral requirements, and thereby the norms and standards by which a person's compliance or noncompliance with these requirements, and so his moral desert and moral worth, are judged. For a person's moral worth can be assessed only on the basis of the extent to which he has conformed to what he judges right, and refrained from doing what he judges wrong, taking into account the care and conscientiousness with which he has arrived at these judgments. The central question of morality I thus take to be: 'What is right and what is wrong?' And since different men give so very different and yet so very firm and passionate answers, a second more theoretical question is almost equally central: 'How do we determine what is the correct answer to our first question?'

These two questions raise a difficult problem which has exercised moral philosophers since Plato. The problem is this. Suppose we have worked out some answer to the first question, 'What is right and what is wrong?' Now to qualify as an answer worth taking notice of, it must at the same time provide a good affirmative answer to another question, '*Should* I do what is right and refrain from doing what is wrong?' In order to yield such an answer, the fact that something is the right thing to do must imply that there are *conclusive reasons for* doing it; and that it is wrong, the existence of *conclusive reasons against* doing it. For otherwise a person might in reason admit that something is the right thing for him to do but that he has no adequate reason for doing it, or that something is the wrong thing for him to do but that he has no adequate reason against doing it. In other words, to qualify as a morality, a system of social direction and control must also qualify as a system of practical reasons for the required conduct.

The problem is how the wrongness of a certain course of action could possibly imply the existence of a conclusive reason against entering on it, even when one very much wants to enter on it. The standard accounts of what it is for there to be a conclusive reason against doing something which one very much wants to do, are all to the effect that doing that thing would frustrate the agent's concerns; that in other words, doing it would be contrary to his best interest, to his disadvantage or to his detriment, in short would harm him, or those about whom he cared. What other way could there be of exhibiting a course of action as being contrary to reason?

Yet it is as plain as can be, in spite of the many theories to the contrary, that doing right (and refraining from doing wrong) is not necessarily in accordance with reason, doing wrong (and omitting to do what is right) not necessarily contrary to reason in this ordinary sense. People are credited with high moral worth specifically on the grounds of having done what is right even when this is contrary to their best interests. In fact, moral worth is much the same as moral desert. It constitutes a *title* to reward or *liability* to punishment. It can do so only because doing right often is not in one's interest and thus entitles one to *compensation* (positive retribution); and because doing wrong is in one's interest and therefore makes one liable to negative retribution. It is a commonplace that people by appearing to be righteous while being wrong-doers can promote their own good in two ways; first, by doing what is in their best interest though wrong, and second, by acquiring titles to compensatory rewards through appearing to have done the right thing. Doing the right thing cannot therefore mean the same as doing what *naturally* has the best results and is therefore in one's best interest, and this cannot thus constitute the proof that doing the right thing necessarily is in accordance with reason.

It is equally certain, though perhaps not equally obvious, that doing the right thing cannot mean the same as doing what *through human contrivance* is in one's best interest, i.e. what is in one's best interest when the rewards and penalties are taken into account. For in the first place, deliberately causing undesirable consequences to follow upon someone's behavior surely is defensible only if these consequences are made to follow for one reason and one reason alone, namely, that the original behavior was already wrong. Otherwise there would be no difference betwen harming someone and punishing him. We would also have to accept this further unpalatable consequence. A person who through ingenuity succeeds in circumventing these humanly imposed penalties has not done wrong but acted wisely, and a person who through innate endowment or training can endure them without great hardship, is not doing wrong but acts wisely in engaging in the prohibited conduct. On this view, we must take seriously Hamlet's remark that conscience does make *cowards* of us all. But surely this is absurd. Hence the wrongness of someone's behavior cannot consist in or be grounded upon the fact that such behavior is naturally or through human contrivance followed by consequences not in the agent's best interests.

This, then, is our problem. To judge conduct wrong is, it seems, to imply that there are conclusive reasons against doing it. Yet it is hard to see what such reasons could be.

My solution to this problem is briefly this. Judgments of the form 'It would be wrong for Darby not to go to Joan's rescue' do indeed imply that there are conclusive reasons for Darby to go to Joan's rescue, but that these are reasons of a special sort, different from those which so far we have considered the only possible ones. The difference between the two sorts of reason rests on the difference between the role which practical reason could conceivably play in the life of an isolated individual and the role it plays in the life of an individual whose actions (or their consequences) make a difference to the success or failure of others' attempts to reach their goals.

(A) *The Role of Practical Reason in the Lives of "Sheltered" Individuals.* What I have in mind here is the highly artificial case of individuals who, though not living a solitary life on a desert island, nevertheless do only things which do not impinge on the lives of others around them. Their lives resemble those of solitary individuals in an important respect: the problems for whose solution they employ practical reason are the same as those of solitary individuals. The important difference is that for the solution of these problems they can consult their neighbors.

Let me begin by tracing the evolution of living beings from comparatively low to comparatively high levels of sophistication through five imaginary stages characterized entirely in terms of the sorts of behavior of which they are capable at that stage.

Stage 1: *Purposive or goal-directed behavior.* When put in a puzzle box, our creature makes frantic random movements which cease when he escapes from the box. After several repetitions, he no longer makes random movements, but only movements necessary to release him from the box. We tend to speak of the modification in the nature of his movements as his "learning how to escape from the box," and of the escape as his goal, or as his purpose in making the movements. The occurrence of learning is an essential ingredient of goal-directed behavior. In its absence, we should not view the state or occurrence at the time of the cessation of the frantic movements as the creature's goal and we should not speak of the creature's frantic movements as constituting purposive behavior even though they stopped when it escaped. However, we should not insist that in addition to evidence for saying that the creature had a goal and that he knew (had learned) how to attain it, we must also have independent evidence for saying that he sometimes had goals which he did not know how to attain.

Stage 2: *Not knowing how to reach goals.* Imagine our animal confined to a cage and placed so that he can see outside it a bunch of bananas suspended from a tree. Suppose that he stretches his arms towards them as far as possible but fails to reach them; that he moves up a box, piles another on top, uses a stick, but still fails; that finally he joins two sticks together, reaches for the bananas, grabs them, and eats them. The sequence of events is such that we should feel justified in speaking of his first few actions as unsuccessful attempts at reaching the bananas, hence in saying that at that time he had the goal of reaching the bananas but *did not know how.* It was only when he joined the two sticks together that he hit upon an idea which turned out to be a way of attaining his end.

Stage 3: *Telling someone how to reach a goal.* We next imagine our creature endowed with the ability to relate, and record in a language, ideas and discoveries of the sort described in the previous paragraph. If, for the moment, we also postulate in communication with him other similar creatures, then a great increase in the effectiveness of individual intelligence is possible through the pooling of ideas. Such creatures, instead of having to think out the solution of each practical problem for themselves, can ask one another for help. At this stage, we shall expect to find remarks such as 'That's the way to cope with this problem,' 'This is how you reach that goal.' We may also find *explanations* of *how* someone did something, i.e. how he achieved his end (e.g. 'his arms were too short so he put the sticks together to extend his arms, so to speak'), or explanations of *why* he did something, i.e. took the steps he did (e.g. 'he wanted to reach the bananas and he had the idea that by putting the sticks together, his reach would be good enough to get them').

Stage 4: *Weighing the merits of alternative ways of reaching the same goal.* We now assume that our creature knows of more than one way to reach his goal. He may then compare and evaluate them in terms of their various advantages and disadvantages. We shall now expect to hear remarks such as 'If I were you, I should not do this but that' or 'You ought to try this method.' We shall, moreover, be prepared to find an additional activity, namely, *justifying* the way something was done, i.e. indicating the advantages or the preferability, over other possible ways, of the way a particular goal was in fact pursued. Lastly, we shall expect to find a new way of explaining why a (sensible) person acted in a certain not obviously sensible way, by bringing to light the merits of his way of acting, which were hidden to others but known to him.

Stage 5: *Weighing the merits of alternative goals.* At stages 1 through 4, a creature finds himself having certain goals which he does not question but simply pursues as best he can, the moment he has them. At this stage, we may assume that a creature can envisage not merely the time span between the present and the attainment of his goal, but can think of what happens afterwards, of what are the consequences of his attaining a given end. He may even consider his entire life from the present moment to his death. If he has this ability, he may stand back from his current mode of behavior, noting the goals he came to have and under what conditions he came to have them; and noting also what consequences, in terms of joys and miseries, the pursuit and attainment of such goals usually had. He may then compare the sort of life this has meant for him with the sort of lives others have had who have pursued different ends. In the light of such surveys he may turn his back, let us say, on wine, women, and cigarettes which, prior to this survey and evaluation would, in certain circumstances, invariably have become his goal.

Where in this development through five imaginary stages do we find scope for practical reason? Plainly not at stages 1 and 2. Koehler's famous ape may be credited with comparatively high intelligence, but not with reason. The solution either comes to him in a flash or it does not come at all. He does not have a systematic way of working it out. There is not available to him a step-by-step procedure which, however long, complicated, and tedious, must eventually yield the answer.

Practical reasoning in this sense, directed at the solution of the problem of what a person should or ought to do, cannot arise until stages 4 and 5, when our creature has alternatives open to him, between which he can and must choose, and of which he can assess the relative merits. In such a case, surveying the facts about alternative ways of attaining an end, and about alternative ends, is considering from the point of view of the greatest possible merit, the advantages and disadvantages of the alternative means or ends the agent could adopt. Stating the reasons for one of them is stating its merits.

This is not the place to describe in detail our complicated value system. It must suffice to say that the key concepts are a person's pleasure, happiness, advantage, and good. It is a commonplace not only that people derive pleasure from an enormous variety of things, and different people from different things, but also that although there is agreement that some pleasures are obtained at some cost in later suffering, there is not agreement about whether all these pleasures are worth their price. It may well not be possible ever to arrive at an agreement about this. We may, however, be able to characterize in some definite way those who will in the end agree that this or that pleasure is worth its price and those who will agree that it is not. With this sort of knowledge we should be in a position to give such people good advice about what they should do in order to make their whole life as worth living as their natural endowment, training, and opportunities enable them to make it.

Let us now imagine a society of people taught to work out and adopt alternative means to their ends, and alternative ends; and taught to ask themselves or others which of various alternatives they should or ought to adopt. In such a society we shall expect to find people at times engaging in deliberation about what to do, both on their own behalf and that of others, asking and being asked for advice and giving and getting it. In such a society there will then be scope for judgments not only of the kinds so far noted but also for judgments of all of the following five types: (i) 'Jones should not clear a track through Smith's woods'; (ii) 'It would be inconvenient, inexpedient, disadvantageous, pointless for Jones to clear a track through Smith's woods'; (iii) 'It would be unwise, silly, foolish, for Jones to clear a track through Smith's woods'; (iv) 'Jones was a fool to clear a track through the woods'; (v) 'Jones is a fool.' The first advises against a course of action, the second states reasons for the advice, the third indicates the (rational) "worth" or "desert" of anyone acting contrary to such advice, the fourth passes (rational) judgment on Jones for acting contrary to such advice, and the fifth passes general judgment on Jones without mentioning any grounds. The occurrence of judgments of these five types is characteristic of the existence of a system of social direction.

Note that recording a certain sort of judgment about him—the sort that we are called upon to make in testimonials—is generally thought to be an adequate safeguard of the interests of others and thus an adequate method of effecting compliance. We do not insist on punishing a person for being foolish or silly or imprudent and the like, though we tend to protect ourselves against harmful consequences by refusing to employ him when he applies.

There can be little doubt that a society organized in the way I have described would have many advantages over one which lacked a comparable organization. For in a society so organized people would be enabled to profit from the ideas and the practical wisdom of earlier generations as well as of their neighbors. The benefits accruing to an individual through his own intelligence and ingenuity would be augmented by the intelligence and ingenuity of all the other individuals the sum-total of whose ideas is made accessible to him in a more or less mechanical fashion. For practical reasoning is a linguistic forerunner of the computer.

But although a society of the kind just sketched would have many advantages over one which lacked this and any other comparable organization, it is wholly implausible to assume that people living in such a society could or would lead lives which did not impinge on one another. Even if everyone intended to avoid any sort of intervention in another person's life, they could not always foresee the consequences of their actions and so they would often unintentionally cause such interferences and mutual frustrations. To be realistic, we must therefore modify our assumption. We must concede that, if individuals are to derive the great benefits of life in organized society, they must be prepared for occasional interferences with their plans by other people's actions. I accordingly turn to an examination of the role of practical reason in the lives of individuals in societies, taking into account this consequence of such a life.

(B) *The Role of Practical Reason in the Life of Individuals Living in Society.* Let us then draw out the consequences of people living in the manner hitherto envisaged; that is, with everyone either following the promptings of impulse and inclination, or curbing such promptings in accordance with the outcome of deliberation along the lines sketched under (A). Such individuals will then modify their impulses, when they do so, in the direction of making their lives more worthwhile, more worth living, than such lives would be if they always followed impulse. For the purpose of this investigation, it makes no difference what each individual regards as most worthwhile. The crucial point is that they will curb their inclinations only when they think that doing so will improve their lives by promoting what they regard as their own most important concerns. And this may include the well-being of others about whom they care, the promotion of art and science which is dear to them, or their own ultimate salvation. Now, clearly, the ends of people acting in such ways often come into conflict with one another. One man's attaining his end will then necessitate another man's failing to attain his. Even if such conflicts were not altogether inescapable, their very possibility and the great stakes involved will give rise to the frightened expectation that they would occur. Such expectations on the part of people living under such conditions—exemplified by what has euphemistically been called the Concert of Nations, the Family of Nations, and of late the United Nations —engender a desire to be rid of the dangers and frustrations threatening from fellow men, so that everyone is constantly preparing for attack or even initiating it in order to forestall and weaken the attacks expected from an imagined or real adversary. On this point, I find myself wholly convinced by Hobbes' analysis of the logic of the situation.

But if this is the logic of the situation, clearly we should attempt to prevent its working itself out to its natural conclusion. For in such conflict cases the attainment of one person's end must lead to the frustration of the other's; and therefore much valuable effort necessarily goes to waste. No matter who emerges as the victor, the total gain can be no greater than if one of the parties had given in without a fight. In many cases the gain will be a good deal smaller, if we count the losses incurred in the fights and all the gains missed through such unproductive expenditure of energy.

It is therefore a good idea to do what all societies do, namely, to formulate rules for just such occasions, indicating which of the conflicting parties must give way and which of them may pursue his goal. Of course, if such rules are to be made effective, they will have to be enforced in order to counteract the natural tendency of individuals to follow their inclinations or to promote their most highly prized concerns. But since enforcement means the threat and, when necessary, the imposition of penalties, i.e. of things in themselves unwanted and unwelcome, it is desirable that these should be kept to the minimum compatible with effectiveness. For this reason such rules should be inculcated with the maximum impressiveness and seriousness. Then they will become not only second nature but also so respected and revered that they will be broken only with feelings of guilt.

Many rules belonging to the mores or (pre-legal) customs of a group are of the sort just mentioned.

Their status in such simple societies as reasons superior to and overriding inclination and reasons of self-concern, is justified by the argument just sketched. If the society is not to deteriorate into a condition of chaos, there must be such rules which are generally regarded as providing reasons for or against entering on certain lines of action, reasons which are weightier than reasons of self-concern and therefore overriding them. Put in this general form, this conclusion seems to me final and irrefutable. It may, however, be possible to show, in relation to one or other such rule, e.g. that marriage is dissoluble only by the death of one partner, that it would be better if it did not exist at all or were drawn in a somewhat different way, and that it should therefore be abolished or modified; perhaps that it would be better if that rule were not obeyed even while it is accepted and enforced by the group.

We may notice two important respects in which self-concerned reasons differ from the overriding type of reason we have just described. The first respect is their appeal to an individual. Whereas in the case of self-concerned reasons, a man who admits that a certain fact is a conclusive reason for doing a certain thing but does not do it, is not necessarily weak-willed. He may, on the contrary, be a person of ruthless determination. But he is necessarily not a person of good will.

The second and connected difference is this. A person who does not act in accordance with self-concerned reasons gets the reputation of being eccentric, foolish, rash, unwise, or weak-willed. But although this reputation has many disadvantages for him, we regard the question of whether he wants to be foolish or not, as *entirely his business*. We may argue, plead, or reason with him, but we cannot claim that he is obligated not to be foolish and no one is entitled to punish him. This is not true in the case of the mores and the law of a group. Whether a person conforms to the mores and the law of the group is not solely his own business. For these are that part of the rules of the group which state what the group regards as overriding reasons for or against doing something. They determine the lines of conduct which it is not merely foolish but forbidden to enter on. They are things a person is required or obligated to do or not to do, as these rules require.

In the case of such a system of overriding reasons, we shall therefore expect to encounter the five types of judgment mentioned before (p. xiv), but also a few additional ones. (i) 'Jones ought, is obligated, not to clear a track through Smith's woods'; (ii) 'It would be contrary to God's will, unlawful, wrong for Jones to clear a track through Smith's woods'; (iii) 'It would be sinful, criminal, immoral for Jones to clear a track through Smith's woods'; (iv) 'Jones was a wicked man (knave, scoundrel, bastard) to clear a track through Smith's woods'; (v) 'Jones is a wicked man.' In addition we should expect to find judgments such as (vi) 'Jones deserves severe punishment.' The occurrence of judgments of type (vi) is a characteristic of systems which are not only systems of social direction but also of social control.

As is well known, there are many different such systems of mores and laws. Different groups have worked out different ways of life for themselves. It is obvious that not all of them are equally good. Some of them for instance violate certain natural rights of some individuals, others impose quite unnecessary restrictions, others unjustly discriminate between classes of the society, and so on. By the morality of a group (or an individual) we mean a certain part of the system of reasons acknowledged as overriding by the group (or the individual), namely, that part which the group (or the individual) regards as acceptable. It is the supreme task of moral philosophy to set out what the ultimate criteria of acceptability are, and to determine the respects in which, if any, actual moralities fail to live up to these criteria. This book is no more than a setting of the stage for the performance of that task.

K.B.

June 1964

Preface to the First Edition

Sooner or later controversies in ethics always encounter the problem of our knowledge of right and wrong. The scandal is that the principal traditional theories cannot provide a satisfactory solution to this problem. They construe moral judgments on the model of other kinds of utterance and are, therefore, unable to accommodate all the four main logical features of moral judgments: (a) that moral judgments can be mutually contradictory; (b) that moral judgments are capable of guiding a moral agent in search of the morally right thing to do; (c) that there must be good reasons why any and every moral agent should do the morally right thing rather than the opposite; (d) that we often know whether a course of action is right or wrong even though obviously we cannot perceive it by means of one of our senses.

As I have said, none of the principal traditional ethical theories can accommodate all these logical features of moral judgments. The so-called emotive theory (which maintains that moral judgments express the speaker's feelings and attitudes and tend to arouse the same in the listener) is incompatible with (a). That theory has indeed an explanation why one single person (logically) cannot claim that a given act is both wrong and not wrong, but no explanation why it is logically impossible that two persons, respectively, should correctly make these contradictory claims, and it must therefore deny the obvious fact that this is logically impossible.

The theories according to which moral judgments simply state facts, whether "natural" or "nonnatural" facts, cannot accommodate (b). For a fact by itself is logically compatible with any sort of behavior: it cannot therefore by itself guide a moral agent to do one thing rather than another.

Those theories which regard morality as a sort of ideal law are incompatible with (c). For the main reason we have for obeying (or disobeying) a law is that disobedience (or obedience) would be morally wrong. But if doing wrong were itself simply disobeying a special kind of law, then we would never have a reason for being moral, that is, for obeying this special kind of law.

All other theories stumble over (d).

The view propounded in this book does justice to all these logical features. On this view, judgments to the effect that a certain course of action is morally right or morally wrong express "natural," if complicated facts. They state that the course of action in question has the weight of moral reasons behind or against it. Since this theory belongs in the group which construes moral judgments as fact-stating, the main task confronting this view is to explain how such facts can guide a moral agent in his conduct. The answer is that knowledge of the fact that a certain course of action is morally right or morally wrong can guide a moral agent, because by 'moral agent' we mean a person who is already determined to do whatever is morally right and to refrain from doing whatever is morally wrong. The real difficulty is therefore transferred from feature (b) to feature (c). If my case is to be more than an empty definition of 'moral agent,' I must mention a reason why any and every agent *should be* a moral and not an immoral agent, why everybody should do what has the weight of moral reasons behind it and refrain from doing what has the weight of moral reasons against it. The reason is that a general acceptance of a system of merely self-interested reasons would lead to conditions of life well described by Hobbes as "poor, nasty, brutish, and short." These unattractive living conditions can be improved by the general adoption of a system of reasoning in which reasons of self-interest are overruled, roughly speaking, when following them would tend to harm others. Such reasons are what we call "moral reasons," and we rightly regard them as overruling reasons of self-interest, because the acceptance of self-interested reasons as overruling moral ones would lead to the undesirable state of affairs described by Hobbes. <u>This is the reason why moral reasons must be regarded as superior to self-interested reasons and why everyone has an excellent reason for so regarding them.</u>

Lastly, this theory can accommodate point (d). On this view, we are in a position to tell whether a given course of action is right or wrong by examining whether it has the weight of moral reasons behind or against it. This explains why we can often tell immediately (as if by a moral sense or by intuition) whether a given course of action is right or wrong: because we can often tell immediately whether it has the weight of moral reasons behind or against it, whether it is in accordance with or contrary to well-known moral rules such as 'Thou shalt not kill,' 'Thou shalt not steal,' 'Thou shalt not lie,' and so forth. Yet, at the same time, we do not of course tell this by the use of one of our senses. We do so by our reason, by subsuming a given course of action under a given principle.

The views expressed in this book are closest to those of Stephen Toulmin, without whose help and encouragement I could not have written this book. I have also benefited greatly from discussions with Gilbert Ryle, Max Black, Peter Herbst, Douglas and Betty Gasking, Cameron Jackson, Dan Taylor, Richard Hare, Don Brown, Michael Scriven, George Paul, and Don Gunner, who may well recognize some of their points incorporated here. I hope they will accept this general tribute as a sufficient compensation for having their ideas used (and, no doubt, often distorted) without individual acknowledgment. I am, at any rate, unable to be more specific, since I cannot now remember what I took from whom and what I contributed myself. Of the many others who have assisted me I should mention in particular Dr. W. D. Falk, whose unyielding opposition has often persuaded me to abandon a point or to modify it beyond recognition. I am also deeply indebted to Otto van der Sprenkel and Bruce Benjamin, both of Canberra University College, and to Miss Barbara Taylor of the Australian National University, who have read parts of the manuscript and have saved me from many obscurities and mistakes. I also wish to thank the Editor of the *Australasian Journal of Philosophy* for permission to incorporate material contained in my article "The Point of View of Morality," which appeared in that journal in 1954.

K. B.

Canberra University College
September 1957

Contents

THE MORAL POINT OF VIEW
A Rational Basis of Ethics

Introduction

Moral talk is often rather repugnant. Leveling moral accusations, expressing moral indignation, passing moral judgment, allotting the blame, administering moral reproof, justifying oneself, and, above all, moralizing—who can enjoy such talk? And who can like or trust those addicted to it? The most outspoken critics of their neighbors' morals are usually men (or women) who wish to ensure that nobody should enjoy the good things in life which they themselves have missed and men who confuse the right and the good with their own advancement. When challenged, they can substantiate their charges only by fine phrases. Yet there can be no doubt that the very best reasons are required, for it is an outstanding characteristic of morality that it demands substantial sacrifices. It is therefore not unreasonable to ask for an assurance that they are really necessary and justifiable. After all, what *is* wrong with gambling if one has enough money left to look after one's dependents? What *is* wrong with having several wives if they can all get along together? What *is* wrong with suicide if one finds nothing to live for in life—if one has nobody to keep?

Suppose it is granted that sacrifices are necessary. Who is to say which individual or group ought to make them? Everyone is busily demanding that others

should shoulder a burden, deny themselves this indulgence, or suffer that hardship, but let someone ask
why a certain person should make a given sacrifice
and usually he will be offered only bogus reasons.
'You must do what your society demands of you, if
you want to get on in life.' But there are many people
who get on very well and who do not even trouble
to conceal their contempt for the morality of their
society. And what if one does not particularly want to
get on? 'You must obey these commandments to please
God.' But how can one be sure that such conduct will
please God? And if one does not particularly want to
please God? Moreover, why should anyone, society or
God, impose such hardships or sacrifices? What could
be the justification for frightening people into obeying certain rules if the required types of behavior have
nothing to recommend them in themselves?

As a last resort, we are offered pious platitudes.
Some authorities will recommend the purifying flame
of pain, the serene joys of self-denial, the searing
ecstasies of renunciation, the spiritual raptures of
chastity, and all the wholesome joys of the life of
virtue; others will speak highly of the pride in having
played the game, the contentment that follows upon
placing another man's good above one's own, or the
strengthening of the character that results from doing
the decent thing; they will probably point to the
humiliation of letting down one's side, the shame of
failing to pull one's weight; or they will condemn the
coarseness and grossness of sensual pleasures, ulti-
mately so unsatisfying, things merely of the moment
that yield forever diminishing returns.

But, really, how crude, how beside the point, how
unconvincing all this is—particularly, when we compare it with the precision and the certainty of the

natural sciences. It is difficult to resist the conclusion that by comparison with natural science, morality is a primitive, outmoded, inexact sort of enterprise. Its continuing popularity seems to be based largely on people's disappointment at being less well equipped than their neighbors, on envy of others who have succeeded where they have failed, on the instinct of revenge, and on superstitious hopes and fears that the Lazaruses of this world will be in the bosom of Abraham, while the men successful on earth will be tormented in hell.

It would seem, then, that there is no case for morality unless it can be turned into a science. But here the greatest disappointment awaits us: morality appears to be incapable of such a transformation. It seems logically impossible to introduce into moral discourse the careful definition of terms employed, the very high standards of checking and testing hypotheses, the prodigious use of experiment, which are the marks of a science. As soon as we import the mathematico-experimental method into morality, we thereby automatically transform it into something different. We are not then doing better what we did before, but doing another thing.

What, then, is left to reassure our moral skeptics, if we admit that the most persistent users of moral language are highly suspect, that morality itself cannot be made respectable and reliable by the introduction of scientific method? How shall we meet the Glaucons and Adeimantuses of today? What are their most fundamental questions and what answer can we give them? Behind all the many doubts and objections just mentioned there stand the two fundamental questions of ethics requiring unequivocal and reassuring answers:

(a) Can anyone know what is right and if so how?
(b) Should anyone do what is right when doing so is not to his advantage and if so why?

If we could affirm that we know what is right and wrong, and if we could explain the method by which we know, we could then remove the perennial uncertainty about what exactly it is that a person of good will is supposed to do. And if we could prove that we really *should* do what is right and refrain from doing what is wrong by pointing to a good reason why we should, we could remove the most serious of all our doubts, the doubt whether morality is indeed a sensible "game," a practice worth preserving and worth conforming to.

Neither of these two questions has, however, been satisfactorily answered up to now. There is still no clear and convincing account available of how we know what is right and wrong. And for this reason alone no convincing answer can be given to why we should refrain from doing what is wrong when it would pay us to do wrong. The chief obstacle in the way to such answers appears to be the double nature of moral judgments. It is plainly their function to guide us, hence the plausibility of those theories which represent them as verbal devices for influencing people's attitudes and actions. But they are also meant to tell us something, not merely to influence us, hence the attractiveness of the various traditional theories which maintain that there is something to know in morality. The crucial moral question, for our purposes, will therefore be the agent's question 'What ought I to do?' asked before acting, asked in order to obtain guidance by moral reasons, asked in order to be put in a position to decide on what is the morally right thing to do. This will be the crucial question because the answers to it must have the dual features which, in the past, have been regarded as incompatible by moral philosophers: the ability to give guidance and the ability to be correct or incorrect.

This question, as will be shown presently, is equivalent to the question 'What is the best thing to do, morally speaking?' or 'What is the course supported by the best moral reasons?' Broadly speaking, these are of the same general nature as evaluative questions such as 'What is the best hotel in town?' In asking this question, the agent is attempting to assess in a certain way the various courses of action open to him. If we wish to understand the crucial moral question, we must therefore be clear about value judgments. This, therefore, will be our first task.

Chapter One

VALUE JUDGMENTS

In recent years, there has grown up, both in philosophy and in sociology, a doctrine which has relegated value judgments to the realm of personal idiosyncrasies. On this view, utterances are divided into two kinds, statements of fact and judgments of value. The former occur characteristically in scientific discourse which is concerned to state the facts, to describe and explain the world, to say how things are, were, and will be, or would be in certain conditions, and to say what makes them the way they are. Value judgments, on the other hand, direct our feelings, attitudes, and behavior. Scientific discourse is objective, precise, capable of being true or false, empirically verifiable or the reverse. Value judgments are subjective, vague, ambiguous, unverifiable by the senses. The problem is to show whether, and if so how, statements of fact can be relevant to value judgments. The problem is, to borrow the title of a well-known book, to find "the place of value in a world of facts."

1 / Theoretical and Practical Judgments

More precisely, this widely accepted doctrine maintains that, unlike statements of fact, judgments of value can be neither empirically verified or disproved, nor deduced from any statements of fact. It is plain, however, that there is nothing in the nature of judgment that excludes empirical verification. A man may be a good judge of character, or of distance, or of speed. We say that he is a good judge of these things if he can usually judge these things correctly. And we say that he has this power if he can get correct results under conditions other than optimum; that is to say, when the pedestrian, reliable methods of verification have not yet been used, as when a person has to judge someone's character after a short acquaintance, or when he has to judge distances without being allowed to use a tape measure, or speeds without a speedometer. Judgment, then, involves giving correct answers under difficult conditions. It involves being able to give correct answers more quickly, in bad light, or without instruments when reliable answers cannot be given without a special skill.

Are there, then, some types of judgment which are not empirically verifiable, perhaps practical or value judgments? Let us first distinguish theoretical and practical judgments. Theoretical judgments are a type of fact-stating claim requiring special talents or skills, such as judging distances, speeds, and chances of success or failure at some enterprise. They differ from meter readings in not being made under optimum conditions, from workings out in not being arrived at by foolproof, easy methods; they differ from guesses, conjectures, or intuitions in being based on a skill or gift, about which we know enough to develop it by practice.

Practical judgments, on the other hand, are judgments with a direct logical bearing on what should be done. Judgments to the effect that something is legal or illegal, just or unjust, good or bad, right or wrong, are directly relevant to answering the question 'What shall I do?'

Commands, authoritative decisions, orders, and the like also directly bear on this question. Hence practical judgments have been identified with them. This view reveals a complete misunderstanding of the question 'What shall I do?' Its proponents must think that when we ask this question we request to be commanded to do something.

But this is simply not true. Commands are not *essentially* intended for answering questions. They can and will usually be given when no questions have been asked. 'Attention,' 'Bring me the slippers,' 'Go to bed,' may be said out of the blue. They are not essentially replies. In fact, commands are only very exceptionally replies, namely, when children, employees, or subalterns are *asking for orders*.

'What shall I do?' is frequently not asked in order to elicit a command or order. When I come for advice, I do not want to be commanded or ordered about. I do not even want to be requested or begged or pleaded with. I want to know what you think is the best thing for me to do. I need your knowledge, not your authority. I want you to think, to deliberate on my behalf. I want to make use of your intelligence, your experience, your practical wisdom. I don't expect you to take responsibility.

'What shall I do?' may indeed mean 'Tell me what to do.' But then I expect you to tell me *what* to do, and not to tell me to do something. The first is answering a question, the second is giving orders. In the first case, 'What shall I do?' means 'What would you do in my place?'; in the second, it means 'What are your orders?'

2 / Factual Comparisons and Rankings

I shall now try to show that value judgments, one sort of practical judgment, are empirically verifiable. Note first that they may be either comparisons or rankings—either assertions to the effect that one thing, event, state of affairs, person, or deed is better or worse than, or as good or bad as, another or assertions to the effect that one thing, event, etc., is good, bad, or just average.

Some comparisons and rankings are factual, that is, nonevaluative and empirically verifiable. 'This man is taller than that' and 'She is a tall girl for her age' are ordinary empirical claims. If we are clear about the logic of empirical comparisons and rankings, we will be in a position to say whether what distinguishes evaluative from nonevaluative comparisons and rankings makes the former unverifiable in principle. It is my contention that the misunderstanding of the logic of empirical comparisons and rankings is, at least partly, responsible for the view that value judgments are not verifiable.

To say that one man is taller than another may be a judgment, for example, when one of them is sitting down and the other standing up. This can be verified by making both stand up, barefoot, back to back. Under these optimum conditions we can see which is the taller or whether they are equally tall. With more experience we learn to make correct claims of this sort even in difficult conditions, as when one has high-heeled shoes, or is sitting down, or is wearing a hat, and so on. Good judgment in this sort of thing is the ability to make correct claims of this kind in other than optimum conditions. We could not say of anyone that he had good judgment unless there were some way of *verifying* his judgments.

Not all comparisons are as simple as this one. Sometimes we compare things in respect of properties which are defined in terms of others. When I say that this house is *bigger* than that, I may base this claim on the possession to a higher degree of one or all of three *other* properties, that is, it is *longer, wider,* or *higher* than the other house. But these are not the only ones. We may also have in mind the possession of *more* rooms, or of *larger* rooms. These properties are the criteria of 'being bigger.' Criteria are properties, the possession of which to a higher degree (for instance, 'smaller') implies the possession of the other property to a higher degree (for instance, 'cheaper') or lower degree (for instance, 'less comfortable'). In our case we must say that the longer, the wider, the higher it is, the more rooms it has and the larger the rooms are, the bigger is the house.

This case is instructive because it shows how criteria may conflict. We have no way of deciding what we should say if one house were longer and wider but lower, or if it had more but smaller rooms, than the other. We have no way of *compounding* these criteria when they conflict. In such conflict cases, no clear answer can be given to the question 'Which is the bigger house?' Yet, there can be no doubt that the claim 'This house is bigger than that' is empirical, is capable of empirical verification or disproof. The mere fact that value comparisons may be based on criteria capable of conflicting can, therefore, have no tendency to show that they are not capable of verification.

In ranking something, we are not directly comparing *two* objects, but are concerned with only one. In comparing, we want to know which of *two* objects has a given property to a higher degree. In ranking we want to know *the* degree to which *one* object has the property in question. Nevertheless, rankings too are sorts of comparison, though more complex. When we rank a man as tall, we assign him the highest rank on a three-place scale, tall, medium, short. Knowing the meaning of 'tall' involves knowing the logical relationship between being tall, of medium height, and short. One must know the number, names, and order of the places on the scale. One must know that 'tall' means 'taller than of medium height and short.' It is not enough to know that 'tall' is the opposite of 'short'; for that would not enable us to distinguish between opposites such as 'dead' and 'alive,' which are not capable of degrees, and opposites such as 'tall' and 'short,' which are.

Knowing these things is enough to *understand* rankings, but it is not enough to verify them. For that, we need additional factual information, namely, the *standard* by which the object has been ranked. Every ranking implies such a standard. Though we do not know what the standard is and can, therefore, only understand what is *meant by* the claim 'This Pygmy is tall,' we could not even understand that claim unless we took *some* standard to be implied. There is, therefore, a sense in which claims such as 'This Pygmy is tall,' 'This man is tall,' 'This child is tall,' 'This horse is tall' are all making *the same claim* about different objects, and therefore a sense in which 'tall' *means the same* in all these cases. Yet the empirical verification of these claims involves a different factor every time, namely, *the appropriate standard* of tallness.

Remember the differences between criteria and standards. Standards are implied in all rankings but in no comparison. It would not make sense to say, 'He is tall,' 'This is hot,' and so on unless *some standard of tallness* or *hotness* were implied. For a tall Pygmy is a short man, and a hot bath would be merely a warm drink. On the other hand, it does not make sense to ask by what standard I judge one man taller than another, one drink colder than another. Criteria may, but need not, be involved in either ranking or comparing. I simply see that one man is tall, or taller than another. I simply feel that one bath is hot, or hotter than another. By contrast, 'This cup of tea has a temperature of 60 degrees F.' and 'This house is bigger than that' do involve criteria. The criterion of the first is the expansion of mercury in a thermometer, the criteria of the second are length, width, and height.

3 / Value Comparisons and Rankings

Still, it will be objected, *value* judgments involve more than criteria and standards. Let us take a simple case first: 'John's was *a faster* mile than Richard's' and 'John's was *a better* mile than Richard's.' Do they come to the same thing? No, 'better' is obviously a more general expression than 'faster.' In 'better ship,' 'better razor,' 'better fountain pen,' 'better school,' 'better man,' it becomes increasingly less appropriate to replace 'better' by 'faster.' A man who knows the words 'fast' and 'mile' must know that, if the runners have started at the same time, then he who arrives at the milepost first has run the faster mile. In other words, he must know the criterion of 'running a faster mile.' But a man may know the words 'good' and 'mile,' and yet not know the criterion of 'running a *better* mile.' In order to know what is the criterion of 'running a *better* mile than . . .' one must in addition know the purpose of a race. If we know that races are competitions in which people are trying to run as fast as they can in order to win, we know what the purpose of races is. It is then also obvious that we must evaluate miles on the basis of speed.

It might, therefore, be said that 'faster mile' is a more objective or more factual expression than 'better mile.' If this merely means that the criterion of 'faster mile' is independent of, whereas that of 'better mile' is dependent on, *human purposes*, this is perfectly true. But since in many cases the purpose, point, or function of something can be quite objectively determined, the criteria of 'better' can, in these cases, also be quite objectively determined.

Take now a slightly more complicated case: 'A is a better miler than B.' Here, too, we are concerned with a competition, though on a somewhat larger scale, as it were. We are here calling someone the winner, not of a particular race, but of a competition made up of many races. Here, too, the purpose of the competition determines the criterion, namely, the number of wins. If A has always won, or won more often than he lost, or has run better times, or run equally good times but more often, or equally often but under more difficult conditions, then he has the greater number of wins, the better record.

Perhaps we are not satisfied to crown the winner merely of past competitions. When we say, 'A is a better miler than B,' we may have in mind all times, not only the past. We then include his potentialities. In such a case, verification will have to wait for future performances. Many value judgments contain references to the future and cannot, therefore, be "read off" now. Unduly preoccupied with propositions of the form 'This chair in front of me is brown,' many philosophers have felt that value judgments are not empirically verifiable because the goodness or badness of a thing cannot be "read off," as its brownness can. No additional difficulties are introduced by value *rankings*. There is, of course, an implied standard, but that is irrelevant, for there were implied standards in the case of factual rankings also. Landy is a superb miler by world standards, I am a bad miler by any standard. But some boys are good milers by college or university or club, though not by world, standards. Obviously, standards of this sort can themselves be ranked as high, medium, or low. The higher the standard, the lower the ranking, and vice versa. A Cambridge IIB is a Tasmanian starred first.

"But," it will be said, "you are forgetting the obvious differences. These value judgments are based essentially on only one criterion: speed. What if there are several?" We have already seen that in factual rankings and comparisons there may be a multiplicity of criteria capable of conflicting with one another. In such a case there may be no clear answer to the question 'Which of the two has the required property to a higher degree?' But this has no bearing on empirical verifiability and has nothing to do with the specifically evaluative nature of value comparisons and rankings.

At any rate, there will be an enormous number of cases where value judgments can be verified or disproved. I once bought, from a street vendor, a fountain pen which he described as a Parker 51, imported duty-free. My friend warned me against buying it. He said it was no good. To cut a long and disappointing story short, it was not a Parker, and it was no good. It did not have a gold nib, or even a proper filling mechanism. When I bought it, I thought it was good, for I tried to write with it and it seemed to work. Later, I discovered that it wasn't any good, for it did not write and could not be filled. It did not satisfy any of the generally recognized criteria of a good fountain pen. There can be no doubt that in this case I *learned from experience,* no doubt that my friend's claim, that the pen was no good, was conclusively verified.

"This does not prove much," it will perhaps be objected. "I possess a Parker 51 and a Waterman. I have had them for many years, and I still do not know which is the better. And it is not as if I had not had the necessary time to try them out. Yet I shall never know." One explanation might be that they are equally good. When, after a long time of using a pen, one cannot discover which is the better, then it may well be that neither *is* better, but that they are equally good.

"But can we be certain whether they are equally good? Or can this never be settled?" It must be admitted that there are some subtleties about the merits of things such as fountain pens about which the average user will never be able to arrive at the truth for himself. I have no record of how often I have had my two pens repaired, nor do I possess the statistics for others; I do not know how well their iridium points have worn or how often I have had to fill the two or how long they will continue to be serviceable and so on. But experts may know; hence experts will be able to tell which is the better pen, even where I cannot. Although value judgments may not always be empirically verifiable by laymen, it is still possible that they can be verified by experts.

4 / Matters of Opinion and Matters of Taste

"But you know as well as I do," it will be said, "that even experts differ. Some doctors recommend one brand of tooth paste or soap, others another. These things are simply matters of opinion." It is true that some such disagreements are matters of opinion, but not all. That Landy is a better miler than I, that Plato was a greater philosopher than Joad, that cars are now better than they were fifty years ago, that *Hamlet* is

*Given an unified standard
that is generally, though not
universally accepted.*

a greater play than *A Streetcar Named Desire*, that St. Francis was a better man than Hitler, are not matters of opinion, but are quite indubitably true. Anyone who maintained the opposite would have to be said not to know what he was talking about. That some value judgments are matters of opinion does not have any tendency to show that all are. If all were, then they would indeed be empirically unverifiable. For it is a characteristic of matters of opinion that they are unverifiable, because incurably open issues. But obviously not all value judgments are matters of opinion.

Moreover, many obviously factual issues are also matters of opinion: whether Hitler would have won the war if he had invaded England instead of attacking France; whether Churchill is more of an extrovert than Mussolini was; whether immigration is one of the main causes of inflation in Australia. Some people have been tempted to say that these are value judgments just because they are matters of opinion, that is, not conclusively verifiable or the reverse. Yet this is absurd, for there are other claims of exactly the same sort which are not matters of opinion, but plainly true: that Hitler would have won the war if Russia and America had remained neutral; that Mussolini was more of an extrovert than Kafka; that the higher cost of imports is among the main causes of inflation in Australia.

It is equally absurd to claim that all value judgments are matters of taste. True, when we are engaged in comparing or ranking pictures, cows, clothes, food, or drinks, there comes a point where further talk about the matter is no longer helpful in settling the disagreement. We simply agree to differ. We part peacefully in the knowledge that what separates us is merely a difference in taste. Nevertheless, it is obvious that a 1956 Bentley Continental is a better car than a 1927 Bentley, even if some lovers of vintage cars would rather own the latter. Even in disputes which are so largely matters of taste, such as the quality of a certain meal or someone's cooking, there are claims which are not matters of taste.

5 / Verification and Validation

"But now you have given the show away," our persistent objector will exclaim. "What you have said just now has suddenly illuminated for me that elusive difference between factual and value judgments which so many philosophers have tried to elucidate. You have proved to my satisfaction that value judgments can be transformed into unambiguous and empirically verifiable remarks. But in doing so, you have also shown, without meaning to, that by this transformation they become, *eo ipso*, something else. They not only come to *mean* something different, they become utterances of a different sort, they cease to be guides to behavior. They no longer provide reasons for us to do one thing rather than another. When we have made a value judgment unambiguous and verifiable, we have turned it into a factual judgment. It then no longer *guides us*, it merely describes something."

This objection is based on an important truth, but it is stated in a confused and misleading manner. The truth contained in it is this. Value judgments and factual claims serve different purposes. In factual comparisons and rankings, our normal purpose is to characterize something, to say to what degree it has certain properties. The idea is to enable someone else to identify it, or to establish laws about it, that is, correlations of some of its properties with others, or correlations between variations in some of its properties and variations in others. With evaluative comparisons and rankings, our purpose is different, however. We are not concerned to characterize a thing, so that people can identify it or can establish laws, but to give rational guidance. We are concerned not merely and not even primarily with the nature of the thing in question, but also with how well a thing of this nature can minister to our wants, desires, aims, needs, aspirations, ideals, and the like.

This has an important corollary. In the case of factual comparisons and rankings, a change in the criteria is of no great consequence. Of course, such a change might give rise to misunderstandings, if one party is unaware of it. You may be using 'being bigger than . . .' with the same criteria as 'having a greater volume than . . .' whereas I may be using it with the ordinary criteria. We may then appear to disagree about the size of a given house, whereas we have merely misunderstood each other's claims. When I say, 'Smith's house is bigger than Gordon's,' I base this on the fact that Smith's house has more rooms, but when you say, 'No, they are equally big,' you base it on the fact that they have the same volume. When this difference between us is brought to light, however, our disagreement vanishes, for it is of no consequence in which of these two ways we use the expression 'bigger than. . . .'

But where value judgments are concerned, the discovery that we have been using different criteria does not end the disagreement. The real disagreement may only begin here. For while in nonevaluative comparisons and rankings we are simply concerned to state the degree to which a given thing satisfies given criteria, in value judgments we are concerned to say more. When, in nonevaluative judgments, we change the criteria, we are simply making a different nonevaluative claim, we are simply asserting the possession of a different property. In value judgments this is not so. Here we are concerned not merely to say something about the properties of the thing, but something about the *appropriateness* of certain lines of behavior in relation to a thing with such properties. Nothing follows about the appropriateness or otherwise of someone's behavior from saying either that the first house is bigger than the second or that it has a greater volume. Something does follow from saying that the first house is better than the second. It follows that, other things being equal, it would be contrary to reason to buy the second and in accordance with reason to buy the first. Hence a change of the criteria in the case of evaluative comparisons and rankings would *amount to giving different advice*. When we change criteria in factual comparisons and rankings, we are merely making different remarks about the things in question; hence people using different criteria *cannot* contradict each other, for they are no longer talking "on the same plane." When we use different criteria in value judgments, we *can* contradict each other, for we are still "talking on the same plane": we are saying that one thing is *better or worse than* another, that is, that there is a good reason for doing one thing rather than the other.

Value judgments, therefore, give rise to an additional question, which cannot arise in the case of factual ones, namely, 'Are these the *right* criteria?'

The characteristic disagreement *in value*, as opposed to disagreements about fact, is the disagreement about the rightness of the criteria employed in ascertaining the "value" or "goodness" of the thing in question. Let us then distinguish between *verification* and *validation*. We have seen that value judgments can be verified just like factual claims, but that in value judgments we make claims that give rise to a further question, namely, whether the criteria employed are the right ones. Factual judgments are decisively confirmed if they are empirically verified. Value judgments, on the

other hand, must be not only verified but also validated. It is not enough to show that, *if* certain criteria
are employed, then a thing must be said to have a
certain degree of "goodness"; we must also show that
these criteria *ought* to be employed.

We can now return to our objection, which was, it
will be remembered, that if a given remark is rend-
ered empirically verifiable and unambiguous, then it
(logically) cannot be a value judgment. This is completely wrong. The question of the verifiability, and un-
ambiguousness of a remark is quite independent of its
being either evaluative or factual. Both evaluative and
factual claims may be empirically verifiable or the
reverse, and comparatively unambiguous or ambiguous.
It is not true that, of their nature, factual remarks are
characterized by empirical verifiability and unam-
biguity, whereas value judgments are characterized by
empirical unverifiability and ambiguity. That a remark
is evaluative does not entail that it is in principle unverifiable or the opposite, comparatively ambiguous,
and vague. It does mean, however, that we can ask the
question whether the criteria employed in verifying it
are the right or the wrong ones, whereas this question
cannot (literally) be asked when we are talking about
nonevaluative comparisons and rankings.

6 / The Technique of Validation

"All right," my imaginary opponent will reply, "value
judgments *are* verifiable. But this is an empty triumph.
What people meant to say was, of course, that they are
incapable of what you now call validation. Value judgments differ from factual statements in just this, that
they *require* to be validated, and that this is impossible, at least objectively. For to say that they are *valid*
is to make another value judgment. And this in turn

will require criteria and they in turn will have to be validated, and so on ad infinitum."

I do not wish to belittle the difficulties involved in validating value judgments, but there must be something wrong with this argument. For could anyone deny that 'Landy is the best miler in the world today' is capable of both verification and validation? Could anyone deny that, at any rate, the criteria mentioned for comparing and ranking milers are the right ones? Surely, Landy's record-breaking mile *is* the best mile ever run so far. Surely, the criterion, speed, is the right criterion to apply. Although it would not be true to say, literally, that 'the best mile' *means* 'the fastest mile,' yet since winning a race is running faster than any other competitor, speed is the proper criterion to use. Surely, here we have both verification and validation.

And what is true of this case is also true of all cases involving purposes. Roughly speaking, the proper criteria for evaluating cars, fountain pens, milers, and so on are determined by the purpose of the thing, activity, or enterprise in question. Knowing the purpose of the car enables us to see that speed, comfort, safety, and the like are proper criteria.

"But how are we enabled to *see* all this? How, for instance, do we know the purpose of cars? Is that something to know, anyway? Is it not something that *we give to* these things? And don't different people give different purposes to their cars? What purpose a car has is for its owner to decide, and to decide at will." It will be granted that we all know what cars are. And the fact that I know what a car is implies that I know the purpose of cars. For knowledge of what a car is, is more than the ability to recognize a car when it is parked in the street or in deserted country lanes or when it stands in a garage or in a showroom. The ability to do that amounts only to a knowledge of what cars look like. A Melanesian recently arrived in Melbourne and observing cars parked at night is told, in reply to his question, "These things are cars." This may be enough to enable him correctly to pick out cars. But even so he cannot be said to know what cars are, if he thinks that they are shelters for adolescents to pet in. He could not be said to know *the* purpose of cars, even though he has correctly guessed one of the purposes for which they can be and frequently are used by joy-riders.

Knowing the purpose of cars by itself is not enough to derive the appropriateness of criteria such as safety, comfort, or reliability. They can be derived from the purpose of cars only if taken together with a great many other more general human aims. Safety is a criterion not simply because cars have the purpose of serving as means of transportation, but because we want to live unhurt as long as possible. Of course, as I said before, if instead of them we wanted other things, then the criteria of excellence in cars would be different. It is, however, a plain fact that we do want these things. There is nothing arbitrary, subjective, personal about it. It would be absurd to claim that this was a matter of taste, opinion, personal preference, an idiosyncrasy, or what have you. On the contrary, anyone who claims that safety, reliability, comfort, and the like are *not* appropriate criteria of excellence in cars simply does not know what he is talking about, or is a little crazy, to say the least.

The real difficulty, however, does not lie in establishing that some criteria are objectively valid, but in drawing the line between those capable of objective validation and the others and, furthermore, where there are several criteria, in establishing which are the more important ones, and how much more important. One way of extending the range of the capacity for

Interpersonal comparison of utility

objective validation is to narrow the basis of comparison. Instead of comparing or ranking cars, we may compare and rank racing cars or station wagons. Then the more specific purpose of the car determines objectively a narrower range and a clearer hierarchy of the criteria. Obviously speed is more important in a racing car than in a bus, and being able to carry a pay load is more important in a utility car than in a sports car. This method has corresponding disadvantages. It prevents me from saying that the Austin Healey is better than the Fargo, for one is a sports car, the other a truck. But this is not a very serious drawback, since there is little point in comparing the two anyway.

If we *insist* on comparing them, we can still do so by ranking each one on a scale appropriate to *it* and by comparing the respective ranks. Suppose the Austin Healey is an excellent sports car and the Fargo merely an average truck; then we can say that the Austin Healey is better than the Fargo, even though they have not been *directly* compared. What has been compared is merely the respective rank in their respective scales. What standards are appropriate for the ranking would depend on the purpose for which such a comparison was made.

Another thing we might do is to draw up a list of all criteria relevant to any type of car. We could then rank cars on the basis of each criterion, leaving it to everyone to determine for himself which criteria he regards as most important. In such a case only the selection of the criteria and the ranking for each are objective. No computation of all the partial rankings for the purpose of arriving at an over-all ranking or comparison is here attempted. The over-all rankings must be made by each individual on the basis of *his own* special purposes or aims. They are to that extent personal, but not purely subjective, since mistakes are possible even then: anyone having the same special purposes must obtain the same over-all ranking, *unless he has made a mistake*.

Alternatively, one might decide to compute such partial rankings conventionally. One might decide to rank, not on a three-place scale, good, average, bad, but on a numerical, say, ten-place scale. One has then made computation possible. The ranking is conventional, because all criteria are given the same importance. This sort of thing is done in the so-called score charts in motor journals. The person testing the car in question has a list of all the criteria he will consider, for example, Styling, Bodywork, Interior, Instruments, Comfort, Driving Position, and so on. For all these criteria, the road tester gives a rank by using one of the ordinary "grading labels," for example, attractive, well finished, neat, easy to read, good, excellent, good for short driver, and so forth. But he also gives a corresponding conventional number, say, 4, 4, 4, 4, 4, 5, 4. These numbers can be added up and provide an *over-all* evaluation. If we compare each ranking, and the over-all ranking, with the ranking for the average, we get a fairly clear idea of how good the car in question is.

I take it as established, then, that there are value judgments which can be empirically verified and also validated.

But these value judgments are nothing but disguised factual judgments — therefore "value judgments have not been shown to be in principle capable of being validated. Baier is mistaken.

Chapter Two

THE BEST THING
TO DO

We can now apply our insights about value judgments to questions of the form 'What shall I do?' For this question comes to much the same as 'What is *the best* thing I can do?' That this is so is obvious from the reply 'I know this would be the best thing to do, but that is not what I want to know. I want to know, *what shall I* do?' A man who says this obviously does not know what he is asking. He may want to query the truth of what he is told, but he cannot claim that his question has yet to be answered.

1 / What Makes Something a Reason?

Granted, then, that 'What shall I do?' comes to much the same as 'What is the *best* thing to do?' we have to ask ourselves by what criteria we are supposed to judge which of the courses open to the agent is the best. It is natural to think that just as a manufactured article is judged by its power to serve the purpose for which it has been made, and for which it is normally used, so a line of action is judged by its ability to serve the purpose for which it is entered upon by the agent. But this is only a provisional judgment, for we can always ask whether what the agent is aiming at is the best thing to aim at. Frequently, when someone asks, 'What shall I do?' he is not merely asking which is the better course of action, *given a certain aim or end,* but which of several ends or aims is the best.

The best course of action is not that course which most quickly, least painfully, least expensively, etc., leads to the gaining of our ends, but *it is the course of action which is supported by the best reasons.* And the best reasons may require us to abandon the aim we actually have set our heart on.

Our next question must, therefore, be concerned with what it is that makes something a reason for (or against) entering on a certain line of action. When we are deliberating about alternative courses of action before us, our deliberation progresses through two distinct stages, first, the surveying of the facts with a view to determining which of them are relevant considerations and, secondly, the determination of the relative "weight" of these considerations with a view to deciding which course of action has the full weight of reason behind it.

1.1 THE SURVEYING OF THE FACTS

What facts must I survey? How do I tell that a given fact is a relevant consideration? What makes a fact a pro or a con, a reason for or against?

Suppose I have been in the United States for some time and have just come back to Australia, bringing with me a brand-new Chevrolet which I am importing duty-free. My friend, Paddy Concannan, offers me £3,000 for it, although he knows quite well it cost me only £1,000 new. I am eager to accept the offer. Have I a good reason for doing so? One at least is quite obvious. In selling the car I would be making a profit of 200 per cent. That would normally be regarded as a consideration, a reason for selling. How can I show that it is? The proof might be set out in the following way.

(i) The fact that doing something would yield a high profit is a good reason for doing it.

(ii) It would yield a high profit to sell my car to Paddy now.

(iii) Therefore, the fact that it would yield a high profit to sell my car to Paddy now is a reason for selling it now.

Another way of putting the conclusion would be to say that *in the fact* that it would yield a high profit to sell it now *I* have a good reason for selling it now.

My wife, on the other hand, advises against selling. She says that, having brought the car into the country as my personal possession, I was exempted from paying duty on condition that I would not sell it for three years. Her argument could be put in this way.

(i) The fact that doing something is illegal is a reason against doing it.

(ii) It would be illegal to sell my car to Paddy now.

(iii) Hence the fact that selling it to Paddy now would be illegal is a reason against selling it now.

How did we make sure that certain facts were considerations? We examined the proposed line of action with a view to discovering whether it was of certain well-known sorts, for example, lawful or unlawful or yielding profit or loss. For we believe that these features provide us with reasons for or against entering on the proposed line of action. We begin with certain beliefs; let us call them "consideration-making beliefs" or

"rules of reason." These are propositions to the effect
that if a line of action is of a certain sort then the
agent has a reason for or against entering on it. Consideration-making beliefs can function as major premises in our arguments or as inference-licenses in our
inferences. The minor premises are the facts which, in
accordance with the consideration-making beliefs, we
conclude to be reasons.

It is, of course, possible to make mistakes in these
deliberations. Our major premises may be wrong: we
may believe wrongly that the fact that a proposed line
of action is illegal is a reason against entering on it,
that the fact that it would yield a high profit is a reason for entering on it. Or the major premise may not
apply to the facts we have discovered about the proposed line of action: it may not be correct to say that
a profit of 200 per cent is a high profit or that selling
a car imported duty-free is illegal. Lastly, what we
take to be a fact about the proposed line of action may
not be a fact: it may not be true that selling to Paddy
would yield 200 per cent, for Paddy, being a shrewd
businessman and knowing the transaction to be illegal,
may refuse to pay as much as £3,000 once he has got
hold of the car.

There is no mystery about how to avoid or correct
the second and third type of error, but it is not at all
apparent how we guard against the first. We learn the
consideration-making beliefs prevalent in our community as part of our education. They are taught us
not as beliefs but as facts. Later we come to realize
that they are only group convictions and that they may
be wrong. But we are not at all clear about how to
detect errors in this field. I shall deal with this problem in Chapter Seven. For the time being, we shall
simply accept our consideration-making beliefs as
true.

To sum up. In reply to the question 'What are reasons?' or 'What are considerations?' or 'What are pros and cons?' we must answer, 'They are certain facts.' What *makes* these facts considerations? That certain (true) consideration-making beliefs apply to them. What follows from the fact that something is a consideration? That someone who is planning to do something of a certain sort has, in the fact that it is of this sort, a reason for or against doing it. That something is a reason, therefore, of necessity always involves some possible agent. That some fact is a consideration always implies the context of a course of action planned by someone.

Does this mean that what is a reason for me is not necessarily a reason for you? In the most obvious interpretation of this question, it certainly does mean that. The fact that Mrs. Smith has died is a good reason for Mr. Smith to wear mourning, but not for Mr. Jones to do so. There is another less natural interpretation of the above question. Mr. Jones may consider the illegality of some course of action a good reason against doing it, and Mr. Smith may believe that it is not a good reason. The view that what is a reason for me is not necessarily a reason for you may be interpreted to mean that neither Mr. Smith nor Mr. Jones needs be wrong—that what Mr. Smith rightly thinks to be a good reason for doing something Mr. Jones may rightly believe not to be so. In other words, the popular view that the same facts are reasons for some people but not for others can be interpreted in two different ways. It may be taken to mean that the conclusions, or that the major premises, of the arguments set out above are 'speaker-relative,' 'true for some, false for others.' The latter view is false. Consideration-making beliefs, the major premises of the above arguments, are not relative to particular situations or particular persons.

It is either true, or it is false, that the fact that some course of action is illegal is a good reason against entering on it. It cannot be true for me, false for you.

This may be readily admitted for consideration-making beliefs, such as that it would be illegal or bad manners to do something. But it might be denied for others, such as that it would not be in my interest or that I would not enjoy it. For it might be said that the fact that some course of action is in my interest is a reason *for me* to do it, but *not for you*.

This objection is based on a simple confusion connected with the use of the personal pronoun. 'That doing something is in *my* interest' can be read in two quite different ways: (a) that doing something is in *Baier's* interest; (b) that doing something is in *one's* interest. That something is in Baier's interest is indeed only a reason for Baier to do it. But then no one would hold that '(a) is a reason for doing it' is a consideration-making belief of our society. We are not, all of us, taught to regard as a reason for entering on it the fact that some line of action is in Baier's interest. What we are taught is that (b) is a reason for doing something. And against (b) we cannot raise the objection that it is person-relative. For it is simply true or simply false, not true for me and false for you, that the fact that doing something would be in *one's* interest is a reason for doing it.

Set out formally, the argument runs as follows.

(i) The fact that doing something is in *one's* interest is a reason for doing it.

(ii) Being polite to my boss is in *my* interest.

(iii) Therefore, that it is in my interest to be polite to my boss is a reason for my being polite to my boss: or, put differently,

Therefore, in the fact that it is in my interest to

be polite to my boss I have reason for being polite to my boss.

Some readers may still feel that there are some reasons which are person-relative. For instance, they might say, the fact that there is good fishing at Port Fairie is a good reason for one person to take a holiday there, but not for another. But here again, they would be confusing the conclusion of the argument with its major premise. The conclusion, like all such conclusions, is indeed person-relative, but the major premise is not.

 (i) The fact that *one* enjoys a certain activity is a reason for taking a holiday in a place where there are good opportunities for engaging in it.
 (ii) *I* enjoy fishing and there is good fishing at Port Fairie.
(iii) Hence in the fact that there is good fishing at Port Fairie *I* have a reason for taking my holiday there.

On the other hand, on the basis of the same major premise someone else may argue in this way.

 (ii) I do not enjoy fishing.
(iii) Hence in the fact that there is good fishing at Port Fairie I do not have a reason for taking my holiday there.

There is admittedly an important difference between the last two types of reason and the others, but the difference does not lie in the fact that the consideration-making beliefs are not equally person-neutral. It lies rather in the place where one must look for the facts which are the considerations. In the case of illegality, bad manners, unconventionality, and so on, I have to look for features of my proposed line of action which would contravene *some kind of rule holding for everyone*. In the case of self-interest and enjoyment, it is not enough to find out that people generally are, or that this or that person is, benefited by or enjoys this sort of thing. I must find out whether the particular line of action is in *the agent's interest* or would be enjoyed *by him*. Only then has *he* a reason for entering on it, and no one else has.[1]

Although there are these differences, there is also the following identity. In both cases, *anyone* proposing to enter on an action of a certain sort has in the fact that it is of this sort a reason for or against entering on it. In the case of illegal and unconventional actions, the sort can be stated without reference to the agent; in the case of self-interest and enjoyment, the *sort* is agent-relative. We must say, 'in *one's* interest,' 'if *one* enjoys it.' But when put in this form, it is true for any and every agent, not true for some and false for others.

Our conclusion is this. All consideration-making beliefs are person-neutral. They are simply true or false, not true for me and false for you or vice versa. On the other hand, all considerations or reasons are considerations or reasons for someone in some particular context or situation and may not be reasons for someone else or for the same person in another context or situation. For a given fact is a reason only because it is a reason for a particular person when deliberating about a number of alternative lines of action open to him. Considerations or reasons are not propositions laid up in heaven or universal truths, but they are particular facts to which, in particular contexts, universally true (or false) consideration-making beliefs apply.

[1] For a modification of this, see below, Chapter Three, section 2.

1.2 THE WEIGHING OF THE REASONS

Our first step in deliberation, the surveying of the facts, as we have seen, brings to light the pros and cons, those among the many facts which are relevant, those in which we have reasons for or against. Let us, then, turn to the second step, the *weighing* of the pros and cons. Our question now is 'Which consideration, or combination of considerations, is the weightiest?' Just as in the answer to our first series of questions we employed consideration-making beliefs, so here we employ *beliefs about the superiority of one type of reason over another.* These "rules of superiority" tell us which reasons *within a given type,* and *which types,* are superior to which. We all think, for instance, that the fact that we would enjoy fishing and that we would enjoy tennis are reasons of the same sort. They may conflict on a particular occasion for it may be impossible to do both. We then ask, 'Which would we enjoy more?' If we enjoy tennis more than fishing, then in the fact that we would enjoy tennis we have a better, weightier reason than in the fact that we would enjoy fishing.

Similarly, we employ principles of the superiority of one type of reason over another. We all believe that reasons of self-interest are superior to reasons of mere pleasure, that reasons of long-range interest outbalance reasons of short-range interest, and reasons of law, religion, and morality outweigh reasons of self-interest. On the other hand, there is considerable uncertainty about whether and when law is superior to morality, religion to law, and morality to religion.

As we have seen, it is most important to remember that the question 'Which type of consideration is superior to which?' is not identical with the question 'What sorts of fact tend to move most people or the agent most?' This is easily overlooked because, as shown previously, considerations are facts and in being moved by considerations we are, therefore, moved by facts. But we can be said to be moved by considerations only if we are moved by these facts not merely in virtue of their intrinsic moving power but in virtue of the power we attribute to them *qua* considerations. The same fact may move different people in different ways. We can always ask whether people *ought* to be moved by a fact in the way in which they actually are moved by it.

We are, for instance, convinced that legal considerations are superior to considerations of self-interest, that the reason *against* selling my Chevrolet to Paddy (the reason which I have in the fact that doing so would be illegal) is better than the one *for* selling it (which I have in the fact that it would produce a very high profit). Yet we are quite ready to concede that many people would yield to the temptation to make such a high profit, for the fact that they would make it has perhaps a greater moving power than the fact that they would be doing something illegal.

Suppose it is granted, then, that the main considerations involved in our problems are considerations of self-interest and illegality. The second step of my deliberation, leading to the final answer, can then be set out as follows.

  (i) (In the fact that selling now would be illegal) I have a reason *against* selling now.

 (ii) (In the fact that selling now would yield a high profit) I have a reason *for* selling now.

(iii) My reason against selling is a reason of law.

 (iv) My reason for selling is a reason of self-interest.

  (v) Reasons of law are superior to reasons of self-interest.

(vi) Hence my reason against selling is superior to my reason for selling.

(vii) Therefore, in the fact that selling now would be illegal I have an overriding reason against selling now.

The correctness of the final outcome of my deliberation thus depends on the correctness and completeness of the first step, the finding of the considerations relevant, and on the correctness of the second step, the ascertaining of the relative weights of the considerations involved. It has already been explained how we guard against errors at the first stage. How can we guard against making mistakes at the second stage? The important steps here are (iii), (iv), and (v). Together (iii) and (iv) consist in the correct classification of the reasons we have. This step is important because our beliefs about the superiority of one reason over another may be formulated in terms of the types of reason there are. Moral reasons have a very high reputation. That is to say, we think that moral reasons are superior to most or all other types. Hence, many reasons are claimed to be moral which are not. For if they are believed to be moral, then in virtue of the high reputation they enjoy, these reasons will tend to be given a correspondingly great weight. All sorts of reasons, from self-interest to the wildest superstitions, are therefore passed off as moral reasons. Hence, too, moral reasons are beginning to lose their deservedly high reputation, for people accept many reasons as moral which are not and which they clearly see do not deserve to be evaluated highly. Moreover, we can evaluate correctly the popular beliefs about the superiority of one type of reason over another only if we are quite clear what are the criteria for saying that a reason is of a certain sort, for only then can we tell whether giving a certain weight to that sort of consideration is justified. In Chapter Seven, I shall deal more fully with this particular problem.

Step (v) raises no special difficulties, for it consists merely in the correct application of the principles of superiority, and this involves merely the difficulties inherent in all cases of applying general rules to particular instances.

2 / Prima-Facie Reasons and Reasons on Balance

We can now review the whole procedure of deliberation. We are setting out to answer the question 'Which course of action has the weight of reason behind it?' or, what comes to the same thing, 'What ought I to do?' In answering this question, we are going through a preliminary stage of setting out those facts about the proposed line of action which are pros and those which are cons, respectively. Every fact which is a pro sets up a presumption that I ought, and every fact which is a con sets up a presumption that I ought not, to do the thing in question. Any one of these presumptions can be rebutted or confirmed later *by the weighing* of the various pros and cons. A given presumption is rebutted if some other reason or combination of reasons is found *weightier* than the one which has given rise to the original presumption. In other words, the fact that I have a reason for or against entering on the proposed line of action *does not entail* that I ought or ought not to enter on it—it merely "presumptively implies" it. That is to say, it must be taken to imply that I ought or ought not to enter on it unless, later on, in the weighing of considerations, I find some that are weightier than this one. In that case, the original presumptive implication has been rebutted.

The term 'presumption' is borrowed from legal language, and 'presumptive implication' is based on it.

To give an example from legal reasoning: Concerning the life of any person, a court does not presume anything. However, one or the other of the interested parties can establish a presumption that the person in question is dead if it can be shown that his closest relative or any other person who, from the nature of the case, would be expected to hear from him has not in fact heard from him in seven years. In the absence of any further information, it must be accepted that this person is dead. But further evidence can be produced to rebut this presumption of death. Someone, for instance, may produce a witness who testifies that he has seen the person recently. In the absence of any further evidence, the original presumption has then been rebutted and replaced by the opposite, that he is now alive. But this presumption can again be rebutted, and indeed conclusively refuted, if a reliable witness testifies that he has seen the person die.

To say that a certain fact is a consideration, a pro or a con, is to say that this fact gives rise to a presumption, namely, that the agent ought or ought not to enter on the course of action in relation to which the fact is a pro or a con. Exactly the same point is made when it is claimed that some reasons are only *prima-facie* reasons, or reasons *other things being equal*. All that is meant is that the facts which are the reasons give rise merely to a presumption that the agent ought or ought not to enter on the line of action contemplated. Similarly, the claim that sometimes the word 'ought' is only a 'prima-facie ought' can be explained as follows. 'Because selling the car would be illegal, you ought not to sell it' means no more than that, other things being equal, the person addressed ought not to sell it, that unless he has some overriding reason to the contrary he ought not to sell it.

In contrast with this, someone might say to me that

I ought not to sell the car now, meaning thereby that, *all things considered,* I ought not to sell it, that in his view no other contrary reason could be offered capable of overriding the reason or reasons on which he bases his judgment. We may call such a reason or such "an ought" a reason or "ought" *on balance* or, following Ross, a reason *sans phrase.*

3 / Deliberation, Justification, and Explanation

Before leaving this topic, we must add a few words about the nature of practical as opposed to other kinds of reasoning. For in order to understand the role practical reasons play in our actions, we must keep apart two very different questions which sometimes are confused with one another. (i) What makes a given fact a reason why someone should do a particular thing? (ii) What must be the causal efficacy of such a fact in moving an agent to do what it is a reason for doing, if such a fact is to be properly called *a reason for him* to do it?

Some philosophers have attempted to answer the two questions by a single theory. They have argued that what makes a fact a reason for a particular person to do a particular thing is that his knowledge of the fact makes him want to do the particular thing in question. However, this is too simple a theory. It cannot explain the fact that we often find out what course of action is recommended by the best reasons without first knowing whether the reasons adduced make us want to do what they recommend. In fact, we sometimes have to acknowledge that the course recommended by reason is one we not only do not want to follow but are most unwilling, perhaps unable to get ourselves, to follow.

In order to see more clearly what is the correct answer to question (i) we must distinguish between three similar, yet importantly different activities: deliberation, justification, and explanation. In all three, the word 'reason' occurs, but is employed for rather different purposes. Hence although the same sentences occur in these three different activities, they do not make the same claims. The attention of philosophers has been riveted on only one of them, explanation. In explanation, the word 'reason' occurs in expressions such as 'my (his, etc.) reason for doing this . . .' or 'the reason why I (he, etc.) did this . . .' and is there used to claim that some fact (which is declared to be *the* reason) has actually moved the agent to act as he did. From this it is erroneously inferred that 'moving the agent' is part of the meaning of 'being a reason.' In explanation, it is indeed true that no factor can be *the reason why* the agent did something, or can be *the agent's reason for* doing something, unless the agent actually was moved to act in this way by that factor. But though all explanatory claims containing the word 'reason' must indeed refer to the decisive factor, to that which actually moved the agent, 'actually moving the agent' is not part of the meaning of 'reason' nor is it a necessary element of all claims containing that word. In deliberation and in justification, a fact may be said to be a reason for doing something although the agent was not moved by it to do that thing, or although he knows that he will not be moved by it.

Let me now illustrate this point in detail. I want, for the moment, to confine myself to deliberate human behavior. For I wish to contrast the use of 'reason' in deliberation, in justification, and in explanation. And it is only in deliberate behavior that all three occur. For all behavior which follows deliberation is of necessity deliberate. The converse is not, of course, true. As long as behavior is not unintentional, absent-minded, engaged in by mistake; as long as it is not a yielding to temptation, a being carried away by passion, a not doing something because one has forgotten all about it, or a doing something under hypnosis or the influence of drugs or because one has a complex—as long as it is not one of these, behavior may well be deliberate even though it is not preceded by deliberation, as when the judge refers to the plaintiff as "the accused" (deliberately, not by a slip of the tongue, but on the spur of the moment and because he dislikes the man).

Deliberation and justification use 'reason' in similar ways. In deliberation I try, before acting, to determine which is the best course open to me with a view to entering on it. In justification I try, after someone has acted, to determine whether he has taken the best course open to him, with a view to determining whether he is to be condemned or praised. In justification, I try to show, after the event, that the agent has taken the best course or that, at any rate, he is not to be condemned for not taking it. In both cases, I am looking for what *are* the best reasons for and against the courses open to the agent. In deliberation and in justification I am primarily interested in working out what is the best course of action. In deliberation, I cannot be at all interested in why I have not got it right, for I am still trying to get it right. In justification, I may be interested in why the agent did not get it right, but only secondarily.

In explanation, on the other hand, I am not interested in the rights and wrongs, but merely in what actually did move the agent. There always is an explanation of why the agent did something, though of course investigation need not always bring it to light. There always is a result in justification, but it can be of two sorts, that the agent was justified or that he was not. 'Tout comprendre, c'est tout pardonner' cannot, therefore, be true. Sometimes understanding the agent's behavior involves condemning him. Judges finding the accused guilty are not necessarily wrong or lacking in understanding. The better one understands a certain sort of deed, the more one may have to condemn it, and the doer.

To repeat. In justification, we are primarily interested in the rights and wrongs of the case. In explanation, we are primarily interested in what moved the agent. This is obscured by the fact that the same form of words can be used in either inquiry. We may ask someone whether he had a reason for his conduct, and what it was. This may be interpreted as a request for a justification or for an explanation. These are very different sorts of request and very different matters are relevant to them.

Consider the case of a posthypnotic suggestion. A man has been told, under hypnosis, to open the window five minutes after coming out of his hypnotic sleep. He acts accordingly. When asked (i) whether he had a reason for opening the window, he says 'Yes.' When asked (ii) what his reason was, he says, 'It is awfully hot in here.' Note that question (ii) cannot arise if the answer to (i) is in the negative.

Interpreted as a request for a justification, question (i) depends on two things and two things alone: (a) Is it hot in the room? (b) Is the fact that it is hot in the room a reason for opening the window? If (a) and (b) can be truly answered in the affirmative, then he had a reason, justificatorily speaking, for opening the window. Interpreted as a request for an explanation, on the other hand, question (i) depends on three quite different things: (c) Was his behavior deliberate or not? (d) Did he know what the decisive factor was? (e) Did he believe that in this decisive factor he had a reason for opening the window? If these three questions are answered in the affirmative, then he did have a reason in the explanatory sense, otherwise not.

Note that there is no overlap of the relevant conditions. Justificatorily speaking, he had a reason only if it *was* hot in the room and if this really *is* a reason for opening the window. Explanatorily speaking, all that matters is that he *thought* it was hot and that he *thought* this was a reason for opening the window. It would not matter if he thought so wrongly. When a man says that *his* reason for refusing to play tennis is that it is wrong to play games on Sundays, he may speak truly even though it is Saturday and though there is nothing wrong with playing on Sundays. He has a reason for refusing and that is *his* reason (explanatorily speaking) though he has no reason and, therefore, this cannot be *the* reason (justificatorily speaking).

On the other hand, our man has a reason for opening the window (justificatorily speaking) even if his behavior was not deliberate but followed irresistible impulse (caused by the hypnotic suggestion), even if he does not know what the decisive factor was (he thinks he opened the window because it was hot, whereas in fact the decisive factor was the hypnotic suggestion), and even if he does not believe that the heat in the room is a reason for opening the window.

To recapitulate. When we say that someone had a reason for doing something, justificatorily speaking, we may make two mistakes: (a) that the supposed fact adduced as a reason is not a fact (it was not hot in the room); (b) that the adduced fact is not a reason for behaving in this way (there is nothing wrong with playing games on Sundays). On the other hand, when we say that someone had a reason for doing something, explanatorily speaking, we may make three quite different mistakes: (c) that the person's behavior

was not deliberate (he acted under a hypnotic spell);
(d) that he did not know what the decisive factor was
(he thought that the heat in the room was, but in fact
the hypnotic suggestion was; for he would have opened
the window even if it had been cold in the room, but
he would not have opened it if he had not been told to
do so under hypnosis); (e) that he did not think that
the decisive factor was a reason for acting in this way.
(*My* reason for refusing to play tennis cannot be that
playing tennis on Sundays is wrong if I do not think
that there is anything wrong with playing on Sundays,
if I do not think that its being Sunday *is* a reason for
refusing to play.)

The first point to remember is that when we deliberate we are looking for reasons in the same way
as in justification. We are looking for facts which *are*
reasons, or which, at any rate, are reasons in our view.
*We are not looking for things which we know will
move us.* We are not looking for incentives or motives.
When we ask other people to give us advice, to survey
and weigh the reasons for us, we are not asking them
to look for incentives, to provide us with motives, to
mention facts which will move us. We are asking for
facts of a certain sort, namely, facts which are properly called reasons, that is, facts such that (as we
believe) if anyone were to follow them, he would be
entering on the *best* course of action. If we are fully
rational, if we are prepared to follow reason (and we
are not likely to look for reasons unless we intend to
follow them, or else we are wasting our time), then
we shall be moved by these facts, and not because
they are intrinsically capable of moving us but only
because, in the circumstances in which we find ourselves, they constitute *reasons for us* to do certain
things.

If, on the other hand, we are looking for reasons in

an explanatory context, we are looking not just for reasons: we are looking for *that person's reasons, his* reasons for doing what he did. We are not, then, trying to survey the facts and trying to make out whether they are pros and cons. We are trying to find out what facts *he* surveyed and what facts *he* regarded as reasons. We are interested in *his* answers, whether true or false, not in getting true answers.

The difference between the two cases is analogous to that between a man who is trying to work out a sum and a man who is trying to tell us how another man has arrived at the figures he reached.

Now, if we do not keep the deliberative (and justificatory) use of 'reason' apart from the explanatory and if we use as our model the explanatory use, then we are likely to think of a reason as a fact which of necessity moves the agent. For in explanation, we are not looking for reasons, but for *a person's reasons,* that is, those facts which actually *have* moved him, whether they are reasons or not. As employed in explanatory contexts, 'reason' seems to imply 'moving to action.' In fact, of course, this is not part of the meaning of 'reason,' but part of the claim made by means of the word 'reason' in an explanatory context, where we always speak of *'someone's* reason.'

The second point is even more important, though a little more complex. It has to do with condition (e): that a man cannot be said to have had a reason for doing something (explanatorily speaking) unless he *believes* (rightly or wrongly) that what moved him to act was a reason for acting in that way. This point lays bare the link between the use of reason in deliberative and in explanatory contexts. It shows how explaining a person's (deliberate) behavior is connected with his deliberation. We can explain a person's behavior simply by reporting his deliberation and its outcome. Such a report is a complete explanation if the person deliberated correctly and acted in accordance with the outcome of his deliberation. If his deliberation yields incorrect results, then we must explain where he slipped up and how this came about. If he acts contrary to the outcome of his deliberation, we must explain why he did so, for example, whether he yielded to temptation or to threats or whether he was prevented by circumstances from carrying out his decision.

Condition (e) is of some importance to our inquiry, for it shows that the fact adduced as a reason must be *believed* by the agent to be a reason. If it were not, then an agent could be moved by a reason without his believing it to be one. The force of the reason that moved him could not then *lie in his belief* that the fact in question is a reason for acting in this way. But condition (e) is a genuine condition of anything being someone's reason for doing something. If I do not believe that the fact of its being Sunday is *a* reason against playing tennis, then I cannot say that this fact is *my* reason for refusing to play. It is absurd to say, 'I shall tell you my reason for not playing: it's Sunday today; though of course I do not believe that its being Sunday is a reason against playing.'

It will perhaps be objected that this proves nothing. In saying, 'James is my father,' I may speak the truth even though I believe that James is not my father. Similarly, in saying, 'My reason for refusing to play is that it's Sunday today,' I may speak the truth even though I believe that its being Sunday is not a reason for refusing to play. Of course, I cannot claim both that 'it is Sunday' is my reason for refusing to play and that I do not believe this to be a reason for refusing, any more than I can claim both that James is my father and that I do not believe he is. But from the fact that I cannot, without absurdity, claim both these things in one breath, it does not follow that both these things cannot be true.

But the cases are not parallel. For what makes the claim 'James is my father' true is the fact that James is my father. Hence my claim 'James is my father' can be true even if I do not believe it. But what makes true my claim "'It is Sunday' is *my* reason for refusing to play" is not the fact that 'it is Sunday' *is* a reason for refusing to play. We have already seen that the truth or falsity of that is quite irrelevant to the question whether something or other was *my* reason for doing something. When explaining behavior, we are not concerned with the rights or wrongs of the case. If I believe that selling my car to Paddy is illegal, then that may be my reason for refusing to sell, even if it is not really illegal. If I believe that its illegality is *a* reason for refusing to sell, then this may be *my* reason for refusing to sell, even if its illegality is *not* really a reason for refusing to sell. Conversely, the fact that something *is* a reason for doing something cannot make that fact *my* reason for doing it, if *I* do not believe it to be a fact or a reason for doing it. Where explanation of my deliberate behavior is concerned, it is not the facts that count, but my beliefs; not the rights and wrongs of the situation, but my beliefs of the rights and wrongs of the situation. Proving the facts and rights of a case only shows that a person had a reason for doing it, *justificatorily speaking*, not that he had a reason, *explanatorily speaking*. When speaking explanatorily, what counts is what the person believed. For only that could "have weighed with him." Only that could have exerted any force on him. Only that could have had motive power. This is part of the meaning of 'believe.' If it does not weigh with me at all, I cannot be said to believe that it is a fact or a reason.

How is it, then, that reason has the power to move us? This is a metaphorical way of asking, how is it that we have the power to follow the best reasons even when this is contrary to our strongest desires? When raising the question 'What shall I do?' we are seeking the answer to 'What is the best course open to me, that is, the course supported by the best reasons?' When we deliberate, we are therefore attempting to accomplish two quite different tasks, a theoretical and a practical task. The theoretical is completed when we have answered the theoretical question 'Which course of action is the best?' The practical task is simply to act in accordance with the outcome of the theoretical. Our question about the motive power of reason is a question about how we are able to accomplish the practical task of deliberation, even when our strongest desires oppose it.

Normally, there is no difficulty in accomplishing it. We would not ask, 'What shall I do?' unless we were already prepared to act in accordance with the outcome of our deliberations, that is, in accordance with the results of the theoretical task. We do not ask for advice unless we want to follow it if we acknowledge it to be good. There is, then, no mystery about why we act in accordance with the outcome of our deliberations, that is, in accordance with what we take to be the best reasons: it is because we *want* to follow the best reasons.

The puzzle is, therefore, not why a man follows the best reasons, once he knows them. For when he starts working this out, he is already set on acting in whatever way is required by reason. The puzzle is rather why people should bother to stop and think, to deliberate, to complete their theoretical tasks. The answer to this question is simply that they have been trained to do so. And if they have not, then they will not stop to think.

From early in our lives we have all been taught to think before we act, not to follow impulse or instinct or inclination, but to think first. We have been told that to neglect this will frequently give us cause to regret our action. We are taught that what distinguishes man from the beast is that he possesses reason, and we normally understand very well that this is connected with thinking before we leap, rather than following instinct or mere impulse. Moreover, we are constantly encouraged or bullied to do what we ought rather than what we would like to do and to refrain from doing what we ought not to do even when we would like to do it. In our deliberations we are trying to work out what we should or ought to do, that is, what is supported by the best reasons. It is not surprising, then, that we are able to do this, for we have been trained to do it even in the face of strong contrary impulses.

The question 'How is it that we *do* follow reason?' is no substitute for the question '*Should we* follow reason?' I shall deal with the latter in Chapter Seven. Here I have merely explained why it is that most people do follow it. My answer is: upbringing.

••

Chapter Three

INDIVIDUAL RULES
OF REASON

In this chapter and in Chapters Four and Five I shall examine the various rules of reason which are currently accepted in our society. In a later chapter (Seven), it will be our task to determine whether any or all of these beliefs are true or false. If we cannot establish their truth or falsity, then clearly deliberation will be altogether useless. For our purposes, we shall divide rules of reason into individual, social, and moral. In the present chapter I shall deal with individual, in Chapter Four with social, and in Chapter Five with moral rules of reason. Individual rules of reason are those which concern only single persons, whether the agent himself (self-regarding) or someone else (other-regarding). Again, they may be short-range or long-range, depending on whether they concern themselves merely with the present moment or a very short slice of the future or whether they take in life as a whole or major portions of it.

1 / Self-Regarding Rules of Reason

1.1 SHORT-RANGE

Enjoyment. There are two opposite ways in which we may feel about or react to what we are doing or what is being done to us, what we live through, experience, observe to happen, hear about, or know to be the case. These two ways of feeling about things can be formulated by means of several expressions: we may like or dislike something, we may find it enjoyable or painful, agreeable or disagreeable, pleasant or unpleasant.

Where these feelings are occasioned by something directly or indirectly under our control, there the fact that we feel in these ways is generally thought to constitute a reason for or against our doing it. That we find an activity (fishing), something being done to us (having our back scratched), a living through something (a bombardment), an experience (flying), a sensation (pins and needles) enjoyable, pleasant, or agreeable is thought a reason for doing it, having it done, living through it, experiencing it, feeling it, and, therefore, a reason for bringing it about or bringing it on where we cannot simply do it; on the other hand, if it is painful, unpleasant, unenjoyable, it is thought a reason against it.

How do we know that we are now finding something enjoyable or pleasant or agreeable or the opposite? To answer this, we must distinguish the case when we say sincerely and without being asked, 'I am enjoying this,' 'This is very pleasant,' or 'How enjoyable this is' from the case when we make these remarks in reply to a question. We are moved to say these things sincerely (that is, not from politeness or in order to curry favor) only if we *feel like* saying them, and feeling like this is part of enjoying our-

selves. There are other features: we want to continue
with our activity, we are absorbed by it, our eyes
shine, we have a cheerful expression, we tend to smile
and look happy, and so on. The opposite is the case
when we find something unpleasant. When we say
such things because we feel like saying them, we are
not making any assertions or claims, we are simply
releasing or expressing our enjoyment.[1]

Such utterances of mine constitute evidence for
another person's claim that I am enjoying myself, unless I am being polite or trying to curry favor. If, in
reply to a question whether I am enjoying *myself*, I
cannot immediately give an answer, thereby expressing my joy or boredom, I might then look for the
same signs by which others tell whether I am enjoying
myself. However, the very fact that I cannot give an
immediate reply is a strong indication that I am not
enjoying myself very much, for if I did I would be
bubbling over with enjoyment. If I can find no indication at all, then it is clear that I am neither enjoying
myself nor not enjoying myself. I feel neutral.

That I am *now* enjoying *a certain activity* in which
I am engaged cannot be a consideration for engaging
or for continuing in it. It cannot have been a consideration before I started, for I was not then, of course,
enjoying it; it cannot be a reason for continuing, for
I may not continue to enjoy it. Only the fact that *I
would* enjoy doing something *if* I did it can be a
reason for doing it; that I would enjoy it if I con-
tinued, a reason for continuing to do it. It is more
difficult to tell whether I *would* enjoy doing something if I did it now than it is to tell whether I am
enjoying something I am already doing. It involves
the judgment that what I am about to do is of a cer-

---

[1] Cf. Gilbert Ryle, *The Concept of Mind* (London: Hutchin-
son's University Library, 1949), pp. 187 ff.

tain sort and that I normally enjoy doing that sort of thing, and also the judgment that there is no particular reason why I should not now enjoy it, as when I normally enjoy fishing but would not now because the weather is bad for it.

How do I tell that I enjoy things of a certain sort? It is comparatively easy to be sure that I enjoyed last evening but not so easy to say *why*. Was it because I enjoy French films, or French films about certain delicate subjects which only the French know how to handle, or because I enjoy this sort of film music or because the color photography was superb or because of all of these things? 'Do I enjoy going to the pictures?' is therefore more difficult to answer than 'Did I enjoy the pictures last night?' And 'Would I enjoy doing this?' involves a judgment of what *sort* of thing doing *this* is, and whether I enjoy doing *this sort* of thing. Such judgments could be erroneous, but most people are able on most occasions to get them right. It is only comparatively seldom that we had looked forward to doing something which we expected to enjoy and which has proved disappointing in the end.

Desire. Another self-regarding rule of reason is this: actions which will satisfy a craving, longing, or desire of the agent are supported by reason. The fact that the agent now has a particular craving, longing, or desire which would be satisfied by entering on a particular line of action is a consideration (for that agent) in favor of doing so.

In order to be able to employ this particular type of reason, we must be able to tell when we have a craving, desire, or longing and what it is for. If we do not know the object of our desire, we call it a longing or yearning. If the object of our desire is the consumption of something, such as chocolates or cigarettes, we speak of a craving. If it is strong, arises regularly, and is satisfied habitually, we speak of an addiction. We can tell that we have one or the other of these by a feeling of restlessness, an inability to work, to concentrate, or to enjoy our current activity or rest. We recognize it as a craving or desire *for something in particular* if we know what would satisfy it, that is, would set it pleasurably at rest. It is an empirical question how we come to know what will set our restlessness at rest. We may have innate impulses to do the appropriate thing, or we may learn by trial and error.

The main difference between enjoyment and desire is that the latter involves a felt impulse toward doing something, the former does not. We may know that we would enjoy fishing or playing tennis or going to the pictures or listening to music, though we do not feel any impulse to do one of them. We say that we have such a desire only if we feel an impulse to do one of these things and feel restless and frustrated when we cannot do it. Eating strawberries and ice cream is enjoyable whether or not we have a craving or desire for them, whether we are hungry or not.

That we enjoy this and don't enjoy that, desire this and don't desire that, are "brute facts" about ourselves. Other people often have different desires and aversions from our own. As a matter of fact, most human beings are very much alike in what they find painful, but differ considerably in what they find enjoyable, pleasant, or agreeable. On the other hand, everybody must agree that the fact that he would enjoy doing something is a reason for him to do it; that he would not enjoy it, a reason for him not to do it. That there is good fishing in a certain holiday resort is a reason for some people, not for others, to spend their holiday there. What makes it a reason for some is that *they* enjoy fishing. It is a reason for *all* those who enjoy fishing.

That we enjoy doing something—a "brute fact" about ourselves—must be distinguished from the fact that we like to do something, which is not a "brute fact" but is dependent on reasons. It is of course true that sometimes we use 'like' to mean the same as 'enjoy.' I may say, 'I like fishing' when I mean the same as 'I enjoy fishing.' But sometimes they are used differently. We can, for instance, ask 'Why?' as in 'Why do you like to pay your debts?' whereas we cannot ask, in the same sense, 'Why do you enjoy fishing?' I like to pay my debts so that my credit should remain good or because I think it the decent thing to do. But I have and could have no reason for enjoying fishing. I just enjoy it.

This may be doubted. After all, we can ask, 'Why do you enjoy hot baths?' or 'Why do you enjoy fishing?' and we can answer it by saying, 'I enjoy a hot bath because I love that tingling warm feeling I get when it's really hot.' But this is a very different question from the previous one. It is never a request for my *reason for* enjoying it, since enjoying something is not an activity, not something I can be said to be doing. Hence the question is merely a request for an explanation of my enjoyment, that is, for that particular feature of a hot bath which I enjoy and in the absence of which I would not enjoy it. I may enjoy everything about a hot bath, or perhaps just that tingling sensation it gives me. 'Why do you enjoy a hot bath?' is completely answered when I have enumerated the features I enjoy. There comes a point when I must say, 'For no particular reason at all. I just enjoy that tingling sensation.'

It might be objected that this is too simple an account. Sensitive ladies can no longer enjoy their steak after the story of the slaughterhouse has been told. This arouses their disgust and horror just as the sight of the slaughter would. That is their reason for not enjoying steak. Moreover, these ladies may have a bad conscience about it. They may feel that eating steak helps to perpetuate this method of slaughter, and that is a further reason for not enjoying steak.

But this objection is untenable. That these ladies would not enjoy witnessing the slaughter in the slaughterhouses is not *their reason* (*justification*) *for not enjoying steak*, it is *the reason* (*explanation*) *why* they can or do no longer enjoy it. The picture of cattle being slaughtered *interferes* with their enjoyment of eating steak. And their bad conscience is again not a reason for not enjoying steak, but a reason for not eating it. That they have such a reason may further spoil their enjoyment. It is notorious that some people cannot enjoy doing things which they would be able to do only with a bad conscience.

In the case of liking something, on the other hand, we can always ask 'Why?' in the sense of asking for someone's reason *for liking it* and not merely for an explanation of why he likes it. That I, as a matter of fact, enjoy doing something is a reason for me to like it. That I like to do it can never be a reason for enjoying it. That I have been given a certain injection or that I have been hypnotized or conditioned in a certain way cannot be a reason for liking or disliking it, though it may well be the reason (explanation) why I no longer like or dislike it, and equally why I no longer enjoy it or why I fail to enjoy it.

Thus enjoying and liking are comparatively independent of each other. There are plenty of things which I do not enjoy doing, but which nevertheless I like to do for some reason or other. I like to have a staff meeting at least once a month, I like to have my cold shower and my run before breakfast every morning, and so on. Conversely, there are lots of things I enjoy doing though I don't like to do them for one reason or another. Thus I do not like to pick a quarrel or to talk about myself, though I would enjoy doing these things if ever I did do them.

To sum up. Asking 'Why?' in the case of enjoying something is always asking precisely *what* it is that one enjoys and never asking for a reason for enjoying it; in the case of liking, on the other hand, it is often asking for a *reason for* liking it. That someone likes to do something is not always a "brute fact" about how he feels. That someone enjoys doing something always is such a brute fact.

That we like or do not like to do something is not, therefore, another brute fact about ourselves, as is the fact that we enjoy doing it or that we don't. That we like to do something may or may not be a good reason for doing it, depending on whether we have good or bad reasons for liking it. If my reason for 'I like to take my Vitagen B tablets every morning' is that I think it will make me strong, then, if the latter is false, that I like to have my Vitagen B tablets every morning is a bad reason for 'I must go and buy another bottle of Vitagen B.'

Want. Is the fact *that one wants to do something* a reason for doing it? We must distinguish two different senses of 'want.' If I say in a restaurant or at home to my wife, 'I want a cup of tea,' then this is rightly interpreted as a request. In these cases I am entitled to make this sort of request and I can expect to have it complied with. In these cases it would be true to say that I wanted a cup of tea. In such a context, that I want a cup of tea means only that I have made or am about to make or would make if I had the chance a request for a cup of tea. It does not assert or imply anything about my state of mind.

But now my wife might be difficult. She might ask, 'Do you really want another cup? You have had five already.' She knows, of course, that in one sense I want one, but she doubts whether in another I do. What is this other sense? Roughly it is the same as 'Do you really desire another cup? Would you really enjoy another cup? Are you really still thirsty or dissatisfied because you have not had enough tea? Do you not perhaps want something else?'

The fact that one wants something, in the first sense, is not a reason for having it. It is only if I have a reason for requesting a cup of tea that I have reason on my side when making the request. My wife is quite entitled to ask, 'Why do you want (ask for) another cup? You can't be thirsty any more.' But if I want something in the second sense, that is, have a craving, desire, longing, or "feel like" it, then I do indeed have a reason. I have already discussed this type of reason under 'Desire.'

Even at this low level of deliberation, we shall often need some ingenuity in order to avoid mistakes. Satisfying our desires will often require a series of complicated steps to bring about the situation, state of affairs, or arrangement which is necessary to satisfy them. Doing the things which we would enjoy doing will involve similar difficulties. Desires will conflict, that is, the satisfaction of one will mean the frustration of others and we shall have to weigh against each other the various reasons we have in order to see which course of action has the weightiest on its side.

1.2 LONG-RANGE

Self-interest. In an orderly society, people's lives follow certain patterns. We do not live from day to day, having no idea what the morrow will bring. Most of us, through our occupations, membership in a family, class, church, trade union, or club, have mapped out for us certain routines and careers, a line of progress from youth to old age. The important decisions or accidents determining the patterns of the rest of our life occur early in our youth. We decide to become doctors, businessmen, or soldiers, or our parents make the decisions for us, or the economic or political conditions of our society relieve us of the burden or deprive us of the opportunity to decide for ourselves. Once our career and perhaps our social status is determined, we set ourselves almost automatically certain aims or goals. We naturally adopt certain points of view, because our position in society determines for us what is in our interest. There are certain factors which would be generally recognized to promote or retard our interests, and different positions in society determine different developments, conditions, and states of affairs as being to our advantage or disadvantage.

There is, for instance, general agreement that it is in our interest to have a bigger rather than a smaller income, to belong to an upper rather than a lower class, to have a higher rather than an inferior position in our profession, trade union, or church, and so on. In all branches of life, there are recognized upward and downward moves on the ladder of success. Whatever lifts us a step up that ladder is believed to be in our interest.

How do we know that this is really so? Ordinarily, we check claims to the effect that some development is in our interest by the use of certain criteria, that it is good for our health, our career, our professional group, our class, our country. If a given development, say the election of a certain party, a trade crisis in some other country, or a war somewhere, answers to any of these criteria, then that development is thought to be in our interest. There will not normally be any difficulty in principle about how to ascertain whether a particular occurrence satisfies one of the criteria. But it is possible that sometimes we may not have enough factual knowledge to tell, as when we don't know whether exercise after the age of fifty is good for our health or whether the nationalization of coal mines will lower the price of coal. Or we may not be able to say whether something is in a friend's interest because it satisfies both a positive and a negative criterion, as when Jones is promoted to be manager of a provincial branch of a big bank, which is a move up since he is now a manager, but also a move down since he is now away from the main office where the really good positions are offered.

How do we tell that something really is a criterion of being in our interest and not merely generally believed to be? The criteria we learn to use—I have in mind criteria such as earning a bigger salary, promotion, marrying a wealthy or titled person, improving our health—are, in most cases and other things being equal, real criteria of our interest. But how do we know this and how do we tell in which cases they are and in which they are not?

The answer is simple. People have certain life plans leading to certain goals and allowing for certain aims, ambitions, aspirations, and perhaps ideals. For most people the patterns and goals are roughly the same: to have a satisfying occupation, a loving husband or wife and a few children, to be free from poverty, anxiety, and ill-health, to live to a ripe old age and be decently buried, and the like. Most people, moreover, have ambitions, perhaps to become heads of their departments, to travel round the world, or to "consume conspicuously." Some people have aspirations such as to lead decent and useful lives, to make lasting contributions to their special field of interest or skill, or to be fearless and faithful missionaries. Some have ideals such as to be just to everyone, to love their neighbors as much as themselves, or to serve their country unselfishly.

We say that something is not really in someone's interest when it would not satisfy or help in the realization of his life plan or the satisfaction of his ambitions, aspirations, and ideals, even though it would do so for most ordinary people. A man who wants to make a lasting contribution to his subject might be better off as a badly paid research assistant in a comparatively small university than as a well-paid but administratively overburdened professor in a large one. Promotion to such a post would not be in his *real* interest, for he would be prevented from making the contribution he wants and is perhaps capable of making, and this will frustrate his greatest ambition and aspiration, though satisfying his minor ones.

This contrast between what is in someone's *real* interest and what might falsely be thought to be comes out in such expressions as 'getting on,' 'doing well,' 'being successful.' These expressions mark the sort of things which are generally thought to be in a person's interest and, indeed, usually are. Most people simply want to get on. They are not in any way frustrated by doing well or getting on—only a very few people are. But if someone is, say, a poet or a priest, then perhaps getting on is *not really in his interest.*

The ramifications of what is and what is not in my interest are very wide. A publisher writes to me saying that he is willing to publish a book of mine on a certain subject, as well as the work of some of my colleagues. Is it in my interest to tell them? One of

them has a book ready on the same subject as I. If he
heard about it, he might submit his draft before I can
finish mine. He will be my competitor for an important chair. Is it in my real interest that he should have
one *more* book to his credit? Is it in my real interest
to get that chair? I certainly think it is; hence (if I am
right) it is not in my interest to have strong competitors, hence not in my interest to tell him about the
possibilities of publication.

There may be stronger reasons still for saying that
it is not in my interest to tell him. It may be my life's
ambition to become a professor in just that university.
The present offer may be my only chance. It may be
one of my highest aspirations to be able to teach there
in a certain way, to promote there certain religious,
moral, and political ideals. My colleague does not
share my views and would pursue very different aims.
All these things are good reasons for saying that it is
not in my interest to tell him.

2 / Other-Regarding Rules of Reason

Enjoyment. We must now ask ourselves whether
the way other people feel about something is regarded
as a reason for us to act in certain ways. Is the fact
that Jones is pleased by what we are doing or enjoys
what we are doing to him, or that Jones would enjoy
a state of affairs or situation or item of information
which we could bring about or let him have, regarded
as a good reason why we should do these things?

Precisely what are we asking? Consider the case of
Aunt Elizabeth who would enjoy a visit from her
nephew Charles. Suppose that Charles does not care
for his aunt, but that he cares for his mother and that
his mother would be pleased if he visited her sister.
Let us say that Charles enjoys pleasing his mother, or
at any rate likes to please her from a sense of duty or

a feeling of filial piety although he does not actually enjoy seeing that he is doing so. In that case, he has a reason for visiting his aunt, because doing so is also *eo ipso* pleasing his mother and he enjoys doing, or likes to do, that. If he hesitates, his mother might appeal to him in this way: 'If you don't do it for your aunt's sake, do it for mine.' This is not the exact case we want, because here the agent has at any rate a self-regarding reason, that he enjoys or likes pleasing his mother.

Suppose now that his mother does not care any more than Charles about her sister. Has he then a reason to visit her? We would not urge him on by saying, 'Do it for your aunt's sake,' since we know that he does not care about his aunt. He cannot therefore be expected to do anything *for her sake*. But there is still the fact that she would be pleased if he visited her, grieved if he did not. Does this constitute a reason even if the thought of his aunt's being pleased or grieved, respectively, *has no appeal of any sort?* If, all other things being equal, Charles were to visit his aunt, we would have to say that he was acting in accordance with reason, not contrary to it. The fact that he is indifferent toward his aunt is irrelevant. If the woman were a complete stranger, he would still have the same reason, namely, that she would be pleased by such a visit and lonely if no one visited her.

Must we perhaps say that this reason merely justifies, but does not bind him, that is, that while visiting her would not be contrary to reason, not visiting her would be equally in accordance with it? But we have exactly the same grounds for saying that the fact that she would enjoy my visit is a binding reason for me to visit her, as for saying this about the fact that I would enjoy it. Since we mean only 'prima-facie reason,' 'reason all other things being equal,' there can be no difference between the two cases. For a prima-facie reason is as much a reason *for* doing something as a reason *against not* doing it. It is only reasons on balance which may be merely justifying without binding us. We feel that there is a difference between our two cases, because we do not carefully banish from our mind all counter-balancing reasons. If we are tired, have other things to do, or have other enjoyments open to us, then the fact that Aunt Elizabeth would be pleased may not be sufficiently weighty to bind us in the final outcome of our deliberations.

Consider a simpler case. Suppose I ask myself whether I have a reason for letting someone talk to me about her troubles. Suppose that she enjoys doing so and that it is all the same to me. In that case, I would surely be said to have a reason for letting her talk and a reason against stopping her. Suppose that she just prattles on without minding whether she continues or has to stop and that I don't mind what she does. Then I must be said to have no reason for stopping her but also no reason for not stopping her, beyond the general presumption that I need some reason for doing anything whatsoever, no reason for remaining inactive. Suppose now that I feel ever so slightly irritated by her talk and she does not care one way or the other; then I would be regarded as having a reason for stopping her and none for letting her continue. But if she enjoys chatting with me, then I must be said to have a reason against stopping her and a reason for letting her go on.

It is even clearer that I have a reason against doing a certain thing when another person would find my doing it unpleasant or painful and, *mutatis mutandis,* in those cases where someone else likes or dislikes, wants or does not want, desires or does not desire, a certain thing. These facts also are generally regarded as reasons for or against doing something. There is no relevant difference between short-range and long-range reasons, hence exactly the same considerations apply there also. The fact that something is (or is not) in someone else's interest is also regarded as a reason for (or against) doing the thing in question.

If we ask ourselves to which reasons, other things being equal, we attach the greater weight, to the self-regarding or other-regarding, the answer is that, if the two reasons are of exactly the same sort and importance, then we always (other things being equal) attach greater weight to the self-regarding reason. When there is a great difference between the two, then the question is sometimes open, as when by entering on a certain business transaction we would gain £10, whereas another firm would lose £10,000 or would be ruined by it. In such a case, either course of action would be in accordance with, neither of them contrary to, reason, though of course one would be the decent thing to do, the other would be selfish. (For a further discussion of these points, see also Chapter Seven, sections 1 and 2.)

Chapter Four

SOCIAL RULES
OF REASON

Some types of consideration imply the existence of social rules. We could never tell whether a given course of action was contrary to or in accordance with or required by custom, law, manners, etiquette, or good taste if there were no social rules to give a determinate content to these expressions. It is only because the law, manners, or customs of a given society forbid or prescribe certain types of behavior that we can tell whether some course of action is objectionable from the point of view of law, manners, or customs and that we can attach any weight to the consideration that some line of action would be illegal, rude, or unconventional.

Our first question must, therefore, be 'What are social rules and how do different types differ from one another?' There are many senses of the word 'rule' irrelevant to our inquiry which, however, have often been confused with one another and with those that are relevant. Discussions involving the notion of 'natural law' from Antiphon to the present day have been vitiated by the failure to distinguish between two senses of 'rule,' namely, 'regulation' and 'regularity.' It is quite impossible to clarify the complicated relationship between the individual's and the group's morality if the various senses of 'rule' are not kept apart. I shall begin, therefore, by setting out six different senses of the word 'rule': regulations, mores, maxims and principles, canons, regularities, and rules of procedure.

1 / Various Senses of 'Rule'

We are all familiar with traffic regulations or with rules of a library, for example, "As from June 1st, cars must not be parked in such and such areas," "No fires must be kindled in the Library," etc. Regulations can be thought up, formulated, proposed, adopted or laid down, promulgated, altered, and finally abrogated. They are not valid or in force until they have been properly adopted or laid down. To speak of regulations makes sense only because they may or may not be in force. For them to be in force presupposes the whole social apparatus of rule-enforcement. There could be no regulations in a world of hermits or in the circle of the family. Regulations divide behavior into that which is in accordance with them and that which is contrary to them. When people know about regulations, they may observe or break them. Rules in the sense of regulations cannot be true or false, and they can be discovered only after they have been laid down. Their discovery consists in the discovery that they have been properly laid down. This sort of rule can be said to apply or not to apply to certain sorts of people and certain sorts of circumstances. The rules mentioned above, for example, apply to everybody planning to park cars in the area indicated and to everybody planning to kindle a fire in the library, respectively.

Regulations are simply a special and highly sophisticated case of another kind of rule exemplified by customs, rules of etiquette, or manners. These are sometimes called 'mores.' When a child is taught to say 'Please' and 'Thank you,' always to look people in the eye when speaking to them, to shake hands with them when he is introduced, he is taught what is proper or well mannered or well behaved. Rules of this sort have not been laid down by any one in particular nor are they modified or abrogated by specially authorized persons. Nevertheless, they "hold" in certain groups and usually vary from one group to another. Their "life" depends entirely on their being *taught* to the young and on social pressures. It is only because people generally adopt certain encouraging attitudes to conformers and discouraging attitudes to nonconformers that we can say that a group *has* these rules, that these rules are rules *of* that group. In most other respects, regulations and this sort of rule are alike.

A third sense of 'rule' is that in which this word is a near-synonym of 'maxim' or 'principle.' A rule in this sense differs from a regulation in that ruler and subject are not different. If something is to be a regulation, it must be supported by some sort of sanction. If something is to be someone's maxim, it cannot be supported. Of course, 'Don't drink beer in pubs after six' may be Smith's maxim and also supported by a sanction, but it is so supported not because it is Smith's maxim but because it is also a regulation. If a maxim or principle is adopted, it becomes the maxim or principle of the person adopting it. If a regulation is adopted, it becomes the regulation of the group. Hence regulations can be obeyed and disobeyed, maxims cannot. One can find out about other people's maxims or principles only after these persons have adopted them. One could not find, to his surprise, that he had certain principles which he had never adopted. If he finds out or is told that he has been behaving in certain ways, say, always giving alms to beggars, this may be explained as the result of habit, but it may not correctly be described as his having acted *on the principle* "Always give alms to beggars."

Maxims and principles also differ from mores in not being supported by social pressures. The fact that someone has made it a rule not to smoke after lunch does not mean that this is part of the mores or customs of his group. It does not become so even if everyone has made it his custom. It does not become part of the mores until it is true to say that to smoke after lunch violates a custom of that group. And this cannot be said until there is some sort of social pressure against smoking after lunch, even if it is only mild disapproval.

'Rule' may be used synonymously with 'canon,' as in 'rules of strategy' or 'simple rules for fishermen.' Such rules are formulations of practical wisdom. Their aim is to furnish learners with simple verbal aids in their efforts to acquire a skill. The skill involved in formulating such rules is not, of course, the same skill as that imparted by observing these canons. The best gamesman or lifeman is not necessarily the best teacher of or writer about these matters. But the latter can learn from careful observation of the former.

A fifth sense of 'rule' is that exemplified in 'As a rule, he comes in just before closing time' or 'Depressions usually begin in the building trade.' Both these sentences may be said to be the formulations of a rule or, as it is sometimes put, of a regularity or uniformity. There is a certain regularity in or uniformity about his coming, or about depressions, which can be formulated in these ways. Rules in this sense are statements (or misstatements) of what is regular in or uniform about something. They can be true or false; they can be discovered. But they cannot be obeyed or disobeyed. In this they fundamentally differ from regulations.

The last sense of 'rule' we must consider is that which we find in expressions such as 'rules of chess' or 'rules of bridge.' Rules in this sense are what constitutes the nature of a certain rule-determined activity. Playing a game, prosecuting someone, celebrating mass, conducting the marriage ceremony, making a will, or supplicating for a university degree are instances of such rule-determined activities. Going for a walk, having breakfast, making a pair of boots, skiing, are not rule-determined in this sense. If I do not know the constitutive rules of such a rule-determined activity, I cannot even begin to engage in it. If I do not know the canons of cobbling or fishing, of skiing or rock-climbing, I shall probably be a bad cobbler, fisher, and so forth. I might have a try and I might be lucky. But if I do not know the constitutive rules of chess, it does not even make sense to say that I am having a try at playing.

We wish to examine the nature of social rules, hence only two senses of the six distinguished just now are relevant here—'mores' and 'regulations.' For only these two senses imply the existence of social pressures in support of the rules, thereby making them social in the required sense: 'wanted and supported by the society,' 'belonging to the way of life of the society.' Regularities are not social rules since they are not even capable of being followed or disregarded. Maxims and principles are not rules of a society but of an individual. Canons simply state ways of doing things well, but society does not require one to follow them.

In classifying social rules, we consider differences under the various "dimensions" or "determinables" of social rules. We take into consideration the way a rule comes into being, changes, and ceases to exist; the way it is supported or sanctioned in the group; the way it is applied; the criteria used in determining whether it is good or bad of its kind; and, lastly, the grounds for having such a rule at all.

Thus, 'mores' differ from 'regulations' in the first and second dimensions. Regulations come into existence by being laid down, mores simply by coming to be supported; regulations change by being deliberately altered by the person authorized to do so, mores change when new types of conduct come to be either backed or rejected; regulations come to an end by being abolished, mores by ceasing to be supported. They also differ in the second dimension, for while mores are supported by comparatively indeterminate and unorganized pressures, those which support regulations are highly organized and determinate.

A more detailed examination of law and custom will further clarify the nature of two types of consideration involving social rules, namely, 'it is against the law' and 'it is not customary.' It will also exhibit the various "dimensions" along which different types of social rule may differ from each other.

2 / Law and Custom

What, then, is a law? In order to answer this question, we must reverse the procedure normally adopted. Instead of beginning with the definition of 'a law' followed by the explanation of the legal system of a given society as a body of such units, we should start by explaining what it is for a group to have a legal system and then define 'a law' as a certain sort of part of that system.

A group has a legal system if and only if there is in that group: (i) a person, or group of persons, recognized to be entitled and required to ascertain whether anyone has acted in a way to which certain rules of the group (called laws or regulations) attach certain consequences, for example, penalties, fines, and payments of compensation, and then to administer (or have administered) to such an offender the consequences affixed by these rules; and (ii) an established procedure of determining whether a given rule-formula is part of the legal system, that is, whether it is what we call 'a valid law.' Anything less standardized or formalized than that cannot be called a legal system. Societies which have not reached this stage of development are prelegal. They do not have a system even of primitive law.

It is not difficult to imagine how a primitive system of law might have developed in a prelegal society. Suppose we find a tribe in which rules are supported by social pressures of an unformalized kind only, that is, by a penalization of the culprit by the tribe as a whole. In a very small group this type of social pressure will be very effective. The breach of a rule in such a group cannot be concealed from everybody, and once somebody knows about it, everybody knows. The "backward-looking aspect of the social pressure" then comes into universal operation at once. No one in particular is charged with dealing with the offender. The group as a whole exerts pressure on him. He is cut or ridiculed by everybody, or excluded from the common food-gathering expeditions and thereby from getting any food, and so on.

Suppose now that it is found by such a group that quarrels frequently break out among its members and that ostracism of a rigid sort interferes with the group's food supply. Too many members of the group tend to be excluded and too little food is gathered. The tribe as a whole suffers. Suppose then that the elders of the tribe, or the chief, take it upon themselves to deal with such rule breaches. If this becomes customary, if dealing with rule breakers by everybody comes to be frowned upon, if the chief guards this as his right, then the first step has been taken in the establishment of a legal system. The specialization in the job of "bringing the rule breaker to justice," the separation of the functions of public prosecutor, defense lawyer, police, judge, prison warder, and executioner, are only further steps made possible and useful by the growth of the group.

There is, however, one other step of great importance, the development of the job we call 'legislating.' Up to now, the only distinction mentioned between custom and law was the entrusting to a group of specialists of the task of detecting, and dealing with, lawbreakers. A change of laws was still brought about in the same way as a change in customs, namely, by changes in group mores. But this is notoriously a slow and uncertain business. If societies are to change quickly, there must be a more efficient method of changing the rules in accordance with which the group is to live. To bring about such changes by a reasoned decision is the function of the legislator.

We can now say more clearly how law and custom differ from each other. Take first the question how particular laws and customs come into being, change, and disappear. It is a defining characteristic of 'custom' that a particular custom emerges as it acquires the backing of, changes by modifications in, and disappears by losing the support of, the appropriate social sanction. It is a contradiction in terms to say that

Jones laid down, modified, or abolished a certain particular custom. Of course, the Prince of Wales, by being a leader of fashion, may "set the fashion." But he can be said to be a leader of fashion only if and because people follow him. Wearing cuffs on men's trousers is not the fashion in England simply because the Prince of Wales is doing so. It is so only when people generally wear cuffs on trousers.

In the case of laws, this is not necessarily, normally, or typically so, although it may sometimes be. Typically, laws are created, modified, and abolished by the legislator's fiat. A rule-formula has become a valid law when the legislator has formally declared it so. It ceases to be law when the legislator abolishes it. The legislator's fiat "binds" the judge, that is, the man whose function it is to declare whether or not an individual's behavior is in accordance with, or contrary to, the law. The judge must accept what the legislator declares law. It is well known, however, that the highest courts of appeal, in declaring certain cases contrary to or in accordance with a given law, exercise to some extent the function of legislators. For their decisions in turn bind those of lower courts, just as laws do.

While this way of making, changing, and terminating laws is typical, it is not logically necessary. We would not refuse to call something a legal system simply because it did not have this method of creating, modifying, and ending laws. The first legal systems consisted of the prevalent customs written up by "wise men."

Law and custom also significantly differ along the second dimension of the concept of social rule, the way in which a social rule is supported or sanctioned in the group. Customs are supported by social pressures which are comparatively indeterminate, unformalized, unorganized; laws by those which are comparatively determinate, formalized, and organized.

Take law first. In this case the social pressure is determinate, because the law itself says what shall be the consequences if one or the other law is broken by someone. Anyone contemplating a breach of the law can find out beforehand exactly what will be the consequences. It is, on the whole, easier to predict for our society the legal consequences, if any, of an illegal act than the psychological, physiological, economic, or political consequences.

The social pressure is formalized, because in order to set the legal machinery in motion and to bring about the legal consequences, highly formalized activities are necessary, such as getting the public prosecutor to launch proceedings, to arrest the suspect, to charge him with murder, to hold a judicial preliminary examination, to arrange a trial, to get a conviction, and finally, perhaps, to have him hanged. For each type of breach of law, there is a well-known procedure, leading from a charge that someone has acted contrary to some law, to a judge's judgment of whether this is so or not, and to the dismissal of the charge or the imposition of that which the law provides in that kind of breach of the law.

The social pressure is highly organized, for nothing or little is left to the public at large. Most of the performances necessary to set the legal machinery in motion are carried out by professionals, by organs of society, for example, the police, the public prosecutor, the judge, the executioner.

On the other hand, in the case of custom, the social pressure is comparatively indeterminate. It is not certain in what way different members of the society will respond. Some may cut the offender, some may merely discontinue to invite him for dinner, others may refuse to give their daughter permission to marry him, others may dismiss him, try to get him dismissed, or merely refuse to employ him, and so on. The seriousness of the response will depend on how strongly they feel about it, on what they are in a position to do about it, and on many other factors. Of course, in primitive societies, where law has not yet replaced any of the functions of custom and where the social fabric is more closely knit, the differences will not be so great. For there the whole group will respond in a much more uniform way. Both law and custom, as we now understand it, are the successors of a state of affairs in which the distinction between the two is not yet drawn. All the same, this prelegal state of affairs is properly described as a state in which custom alone prevails, even though custom has here a more uniform and more efficient sanction than in our society.

In contrast with law, social pressures supporting customs are not formalized; there are no special formalized procedures to set any machinery in motion. Every member of the society acts spontaneously.

Lastly, the social pressures supporting customs are not organized, that is to say, no special organs of society are entrusted with the job of exerting the social pressure. Anyone and everyone responds in certain ways to the breach of an established custom.

There are no important differences in the way laws and customs are applied. It is part of the content of a law or custom to specify the groups of persons to whom it is meant to apply. Ex-servicemen's preference, military draft regulations, aliens' registration regulations, the custom that men should take their hats off in lifts, that they walk on that side of a lady which is nearer the gutter, that young girls should not wear make-up or go out with boys without a chaperone, from their very nature apply to certain groups of persons only.

It would lead too far afield to enumerate the criteria of good and bad laws or customs. It must suffice here to say that by and large they are similar. In both cases, we are mainly concerned with the desirability from one point of view or another of having just this particular practice or that *made universal* in the group. There are, however, certain special considerations in the case of laws, due to the fact that these are made by legislators. Hence we can ask—what we cannot ask in the case of customs—how well made the laws are, how clearly and fairly they are drawn up, and how well they are achieving the legislator's purpose.

Again, roughly the same considerations are used to justify our having customs and laws at all. Living outside groups with a common way of life would be living in a state in which, as Hobbes claimed, life is "solitary, poor, nasty, brutish, and short," if possible at all. However, to remedy this it is not necessary, as Hobbes claimed, to impose laws on men. Customs are enough to meet the need pointed out by Hobbes. Law needs an additional justification which is not hard to find. The main advantage of laws over customs is that a group of well-informed persons can meet the problems and difficulties confronting the group in the conditions of rapid social changes by a deliberate and immediate correction of certain harmful details in the way of life of the whole group.

3 / Religion

For the sake of comparison, let me add a few words about one other type of consideration involving rules, namely, the consideration that something is against one's religion, that it is sinful or contrary to the will of God. It is impossible, in this book, to speak about religion in general. For that would involve speaking not only about the Christian religion but also about how far a social institution may differ from it and still be called a religion. Christianity, which must serve as our model of religion as such, is a system of supernatural beliefs and rules supported by supernatural sanctions modeled on an earthly legal system. The world picture conveyed is that of a cosmic society created and ruled by a divine and perfect ruler, legislator, judge, and controller of prisons, who governs the world in accordance with his own law or plan. Human beings, his creatures, children, and subjects, are capable of glimpsing parts of this divine law and plan because of a certain faculty of cognizing it, the faculty of reason or "the natural light," and also because God, in his wisdom, has revealed this law to Moses on Mt. Sinai. Our religion claims to put us in possession of a higher sort of law supported by a higher and more perfectly working sort of sanction. Christianity, therefore, implies a composite world picture: that of an omnipotent magician who, by his fiat, creates things, that of a loving and just father issuing orders, and that of an omniscient and just legislator, judge, and executioner. The full implications of our religion are, therefore, incomprehensible to people who are at a prelegal stage of development, for this religion of ours involves the notions of 'law,' 'judge,' 'damnation,' all of which make sense only within a legal framework. Hence religious considerations, as we understand them, are nothing but special sorts of legal considerations.

There is, however, one important difference which will occupy us when discussing moral considerations. Law is a social phenomenon in every sense. There can be no personal laws, no personal legal convictions. The ordinary individual cannot have his own laws, his own legal convictions, his own verdicts or sentences. The expressions 'my law,' 'my verdict,' 'my sentence' can mean only 'law which I made,' 'verdict which I gave,' 'sentence which I passed,' and these activities are properly performed by the social organs specially entrusted with these tasks. The individual has simply to learn what *are* the laws of his society, and he has to conform to them. He can, through his own political activity, exercise a certain amount of pressure on the legislative organs, but that is all. For the rest he is simply subject to the existing legal system.

This is not so in the case of religion. True, the individual first absorbs his religion from his environment. He is taught the faith of his parents or his schoolteachers. But later, he may become a convert, or even invent his own creed. It does not make sense to say that a man has become a convert to another legal system. He can, of course, favor another legal system and work for its adoption, but he cannot simply become a member of that legal system by deciding to do so. A man can become a member (the sole member) of a hitherto nonexisting religion. A man cannot become a member of a hitherto nonexisting legal system.

The word 'custom' is ambiguous. We may use it to mean individual or social custom. 'It is my custom to smoke after lunch' or 'to drink wine with my meals' or 'to shave every morning' is perfectly compatible with the fact that I am the only one whose custom this is. It is also compatible with the fact that in my country it is not customary to do these things. In this case, if my customs were known, I would probably be called unconventional and treated accordingly.

However, it is important to stress that there is a logical gap between these two uses. If everyone in a group is a Christian, then the religion of the group is

Christianity. But if everyone smokes after meals, then it is not necessarily the custom of the group to smoke after meals. It is only if not smoking after meals is in some way *contrary to custom* that smoking after meals has become the custom, or customary. It may, indeed, be the case that if almost every member of the group were a Christian considerable pressure would be exerted on the few atheists and Mohammedans to become Christians also. But this is not by any means logically necessary or even desirable. An excellent case can be made for religious tolerance. However, it does not even make sense to attempt to make a case for legal tolerance. There is an obvious sense in which everyone is himself the final authority on religion. In the same sense, the legislator is the final authority on law, the group as a whole on custom.

One further point. It is obviously possible to ascertain whether a given course of action is or is not contrary to custom, good manners, etiquette, or the law. It makes sense to say, 'It is (not) true that belching after meals is rude, unconventional, contrary to custom, illegal.' But it would not occur to anyone to ask whether the custom, convention, rule, or law against belching was true or not true. The only question we can ask at this level is whether the custom, convention, rule, or law is good or bad, civilized or uncivilized, desirable or undesirable.

Social rules of reason, then, are those involving custom, law, manners, etiquette, conventions, traditions. It is a social rule of reason accepted in our society that actions which are required by custom, law, manners, etiquette, conventions, and traditions have the support of reason, those which are prohibited by them are rejected by reason. That a line of action is required by one or all of these is, therefore, accepted as a pro; that it is prohibited, as a con.

Chapter Five

MORAL REASONS

We can now turn to the question of what are moral reasons or considerations, as opposed to those other kinds which we have already examined. They are obviously those which occur in moral deliberation and the occurrence of which makes deliberation moral. We say of someone that he is a person of good will if he is always prepared (should it be necessary) to enter, before acting, into moral deliberation, that is to say, to work out what is, morally speaking, the best course open to him, that is, the course supported by the best moral reasons, and also prepared to act in accordance with the outcome of such deliberations.

What we normally call our moral convictions function as moral rules of reason, as moral consideration-making beliefs. Ordinarily, of course, our moral convictions are formulated simply as 'Stealing is wrong,' 'Lying is wrong,' and so on. They are not normally stated in the form I have given them, namely, 'The

fact that stealing is wrong is a reason against stealing.'
Nevertheless, although they are not formulated in this
way, they are used as moral rules of reason. Just as
we call those things dictated by self-interest reasons
of self-interest, so we call those things dictated by
morality moral reasons. To say that something is morally wrong is merely another way of saying that it is
prohibited by, that it is against or contrary to, morality. Hence in the fact that something is wrong one
has a reason (a moral one) against doing it. If something is a case of stealing and if stealing is wrong,
that is, contrary to morality, then one has a moral
reason against doing that thing.

1 / Moral Convictions Can Be True or False

It is often argued that our moral convictions are
merely expressions of our feelings, emotions, or attitudes, or that they are commands or pseudo commands, and that, therefore, they cannot be true or
false. It might be added that they must have some
kind of imperatival force, for it must be possible to
act in accordance with or contrary to them. But one
cannot act in accordance with or contrary to truths or
facts. Truths or facts are compatible with any sort of
behavior. Truths are, therefore, useless in morality.
There we need something in the nature of precepts.

This argument is unsound. It is not impossible for
a remark to be true or false and also imperatival. If,
in a train, I say to my neighbor, 'No smoking in here,'
I say something which can be true or false (for it may
or may not be a nonsmokers') and also imperatival
(for if it is a nonsmokers', then there is a rule forbidding
smoking in the compartment). Thus, what makes 'No
smoking in here' and 'Smoking prohibited' capable of
being true or false is the fact that these remarks imply
the existence and authority of certain orders or rules.

Thus 'No smoking in here' can be true (or false), because the rule 'No smoking in this compartment' may be properly laid down by the Railway Company which may be entitled to do so. Our main task will, of course, be to show what are the appropriate tests which a moral rule must pass in order that remarks implying its existence should be said to be true. We have to answer questions such as what are the tests which the rule 'Thou shalt not kill' must pass if it is to be true that killing is wrong.

The proof that moral convictions could be true or false and also imperatival seems to me to constitute quite a strong argument in favor of saying that they actually are true or false, for this is what we all naturally think. The only reason why we have doubts is that philosophers have various reasons for saying that propositions cannot be both imperatival and true or false. However, in view of the great popularity of the emotive and imperativalist theories, it is perhaps not out of place to devote some additional space to establishing this conclusion.

My main contention is that we could not properly speak of *a morality*, as opposed to a system of conventions, customs, or laws, unless the question of the correctness or incorrectness, truth or falsity, of the rules prevalent in a community is asked, unless, in other words, the prevalent rules are subjected to certain tests. It is only when the current rules are no longer regarded as sacrosanct, as incapable of alteration or improvement, only when the current rules are contrasted with other possible, improved, ideal rules, that a group can be said to have a morality as opposed to a mere set of taboos.

We distinguish a great many different moralities— Greek, Roman, Arapesh, Christian, Mohammedan, Communist, feudal, bourgeois, proletarian, and so on.

Moralities are always someone's, whether an individual's or a group's. In these respects, moralities are like customs and legal systems.[1] But in another respect, moralities on the one hand and legal systems and customs on the other differ radically. When we have settled whether a line of action is in accordance with or contrary to the law or the customs of the group in question, we have settled conclusively whether this line of action is lawful or unlawful, customary or not customary. We cannot go on to ask, 'Well, perhaps it is legal here or customary there, but is it *really* legal, is it *really* customary?' Nor does it make sense to say, 'There is no law or custom against this sort of thing anywhere, but perhaps this sort of thing is *really* illegal or *really* contrary to custom.' By contrast, this kind of distinction can be and is drawn in moral matters. When we hear that in certain countries virginity above a certain age is regarded as selfish and immoral, or that not having scalped anyone by a certain age is regarded as cowardly or slothful, or that it is "wrong" for women to pass a certain stone without veiling their faces, we do not think that the question whether these sorts of conduct are *really* wrong has been decisively settled. Even whether these things are *wrong in that country* has not been answered. It has only been established that these types of conduct are *believed wrong in that country*.

When we have settled that something is against the customs or laws of a certain group, we cannot go on to ask whether it is merely believed or actually known to be illegal or contrary to custom. A person who goes on to ask that question must be said not to know what he is talking about. On the other hand, a person likewise does not know what he is talking about if he

[1] For a modification, see above, Chapter Four, section 3, p. 79.

believes that finding out whether some course of action is contrary to the morality of a certain group settles the question whether this course of action is morally wrong. For he ignores the crucial question 'Is what the morality of that group forbids *really* wrong?' or, put differently, 'Are the moral convictions of that group true?' I take it for granted, then, that ordinary usage draws just that distinction between morality on the one hand and the custom and law on the other.

But, it might be asked, what does that prove? Our language might be confused. Perhaps we allow that question without having provided a method of answering it. Our moral locutions may be the embodiment of wishful thinking. It is not enough to point out that we *ask*, 'But are the moral convictions of this group really true?' If that question is to make sense, a procedure for answering it has to exist and it must be a sensible one.

I agree with the principle behind this objection. It is not enough to show, for instance, that we frequently do ask the question 'But is this religion true?' If it were enough, certain modern analyses of religious language would be obviously false. Certain philosophers who say that religious language is purely evocative could then be refuted simply by the reminder "But we do ask the question 'Is his religion true?' and your analysis does not permit it to be asked." Or when other philosophers say that the claim 'God exists' is a complex empirical assertion implying that things will not go from bad to worse in the future, but will in the end be all right, they could be refuted simply by saying that this is not implied in the religious assertion that God exists. I do not think that such philosophers can be so easily refuted. A refutation would have to show not only that we all *think* that this is not implied in such remarks or that we all wish to ask whether such remarks are true, but also that what we imply or what we wish to ask is sensible, that there is room for this question, that we can sensibly imply what we intend to, that we can ask this question and imply what we intend without making nonsense of our religious assertions. It is just because this is so difficult that some philosophers have been driven into these alternative analyses of religious assertions.

This is true of moral claims also. It is not enough to say, 'But we *do* ask whether our moral convictions are true.' We must also show what exactly is the sense of this question and how exactly it can be answered. When this is shown, as I shall do presently (in Chapters Five and Seven), our original claim has been made good. Since we want to ask whether our moral convictions are true and since it can be explained what this question means and how it is answered and since it can be shown that it is an eminently sensible question, there can no longer be any objection to allowing it.

It follows from this that one of the most popular models of the nature of morality, the conception of it as divine or natural law, is inappropriate. Admittedly, at first sight, the notion of law looks promising. Like its moral analogue, the question whether something is in accordance with or contrary to law is completely objective: everybody within or outside a given society could be wrong about the legality or illegality of a given line of conduct. An enterprising lawyer may unearth an old law that is relevant. Before his find everyone including himself might well have considered that line of action lawful. His discovery shows that this universal belief was false. In this respect law is much closer to morality than custom. For if everyone in a certain society *believes* that something is contrary to custom, then it *necessarily* is. We all think it customary for gentlemen to take off their hats when the national anthem is played, hence it *is* customary. Not so with law, or with morality.

Nevertheless, the concept of law does not fit the case of morality. The very feature that makes it so attractive to religious persons renders it unsuitable as a model of morality. Religious people like to think of morality as a sort of law, because law implies or at any rate strongly suggests a legislator. If morality is a perfect law, then there must be a perfect legislator: God. But this is precisely the objection to law as a model of morality. For a legislator authoritatively settles the question whether a type of conduct is lawful or otherwise: *he makes it so.* The legality or illegality of a type of action is the logical consequence of the legislator's decision. It is the very function of the legislator to bring into being or abolish the illegality of something, as he thinks fit. However, the rightness or wrongness of a type of action cannot be the logical consequence of anyone's decision. An omniscient person would indeed *know* the difference between right and wrong and could reliably inform us of it, but he can only show us where the line runs—he cannot draw it. It is nonsense to say, 'Yesterday God decreed that killing shall no longer be morally wrong' or 'The moral law against lying was promulgated on May 1st.' Morality, therefore, cannot be any sort of law.

It must not be inferred from this that legal systems cannot be criticized on moral grounds. Even though the legislator is entitled to make whatever laws he thinks fit and even though whatever he enacts is really law, and even though it is true that there is no super-law with which the legislator must attempt to make his own enactments agree, nevertheless the legal enactments are open to criticism *from the moral point of view.*

The same point can also be made in the following way. Law and morality have this in common: everyone in this country can be wrong about this or that type of action being legal or illegal, right or wrong. This distinguishes both law and morality from mere custom. It is therefore more plausible to say that morality is a sort of law than to say that it is just convention. All the same, it is misleading. For when it has been established that adultery, say, is permitted by our law, then no further mistake is logically possible, in the field of law. It is then certain that in our country adultery is not unlawful. Incorporation of a rule in the legal system of a country is a final guarantee of the legality or illegality of the type of conduct in question. The law of the group cannot be illegal. It might perhaps be said against this that the law can be illegal when there is a constitution. But then my point can be made by saying that the constitution can't be unconstitutional. On the other hand, embodiment in the morality of the group is no final guarantee of the morality or immorality of the type of conduct in question. The morality of the group may be wrong. The moral convictions of the group may be mistaken.

I take it as established, then, that it is the very meaning of 'a morality' that it should contain a body of moral convictions which can be true or false, that is, a body of rules or precepts for which there are certain tests. If this is true, then morality is a comparatively sophisticated system of rules, and we have to admit the possibility of nonmoral or premoral societies, just as there are nonpolitical or prepolitical societies, such as the Australian aborigines. I believe that, as a matter of fact, moralities have appeared for the first time at roughly the stage when religion superseded magic (or whatever else may have preceded it) and law began to be added to custom. At that time, I believe, morality developed out of taboo. The main step in that direction is the dim realization, expressed in the powers given to a legislator, that the group's way of life is not altogether sacrosanct. The slow, unthought-out, uncontrolled way of social change is superseded by the method of deliberate, thought-out, sudden changes introduced by the legislator. At the same time, it is understood that the legislator is capable of making mistakes, that his legislation is not arbitrary, but is supposed to aim at certain things. In the absence of a clear understanding of what he is supposed to be aiming at, it seems a plausible thing to say that he is aiming at The Perfect Law which is laid up in heaven. But, as we have seen, on closer inspection, this is not satisfactory. As long as we are dealing with a legislator and his law, the same question necessarily arises: what are the grounds on which the legislator, however perfect he may be, is drawing up his legislation? Until these grounds are found, we cannot tell of any piece of legislation or its author whether it or he is perfect. And when we know the grounds, we no longer need, as a sitter for our legislative portrait, the perfect legislator and his law.

2 / The Moral Point of View

What, then, is the test which a moral conviction must pass in order to be called true? Many philosophers have held that there is not and cannot be such a test. They would perhaps admit that we may reduce our moral convictions to a few basic moral principles, or perhaps even only one, from which all others can be derived, but they would hold that at least one such principle must simply be selected as we please. Such basic principles, they would say, are matters for deciding, not for finding out.

I shall argue, on the contrary, that our moral convictions are true if they can be seen to be required or acceptable *from the moral point of view*. It is indeed true that a person must adopt the moral point of view if he is to be moral. But it is not true that this is an arbitrary decision. On the contrary, I shall show, in Chapter Seven, that there are the very best reasons for adopting this point of view.

Answers to practical questions can be arrived at by reference to a point of view, which may be defined by a principle. When we adopt a certain point of view, we adopt its defining principle. To look at practical problems from that point of view is to be prepared to answer practical questions of the form 'What shall I do?' 'What should be done?' by reference to its defining principle.

Suppose the problem under discussion is whether or not a certain traffic roundabout should be erected at a certain intersection. I can look at this from various points of view, that of a pedestrian or a motorist, a local politician or a manufacturer of roundabouts, and so on. In cases such as these, we have in mind the demands, goals, or aims of persons holding certain special positions or jobs or functions in a society. To look at our problem from the point of view of a motorist is to ask whether the erection of a roundabout at this intersection is in the interest of a motorist. For different points of view there may, of course, be different, even opposing, answers to the same practical questions. The roundabout may be in the interest of a motorist but not of a pedestrian, in the interest of a manufacturer of roundabouts but not of a local politician who depends for his votes on the poorer section (the pedestrians) of the population.

A point of view is not necessarily defined by the principle of self-interest or its more specific application to a particular position in society. We can, for instance, look at this problem from the point of view of town planners or traffic experts, who may favor the roundabout because their special task is to solve traffic problems. Their point of view is defined by the principle 'Favor anything that keeps the traffic flowing; oppose anything that is likely to cause traffic holdups.' But the erection of the roundabout can hardly be said to be *in their interest*. They do not derive any personal advantage or benefit from the scheme. There are many such disinterested points of view, for example, the point of view of a social worker, a social reformer, an advocate of public health schemes, a missionary.

A person is of good will if he adopts the moral point of view as supreme, that is, as overriding all other points of view. When asking the question 'What shall I do?' or 'What is to be done?' such a person will always engage in moral deliberation, survey and weigh the moral considerations, and give them greater weight than any others. A person has adopted the moral point of view when he reviews the facts in the light of *his* moral convictions. We do not require him to test his moral convictions every time, but only because we presume that he already has true moral convictions. This presumption may be false. He may simply have accepted without much questioning the moral convictions of his group, or he may have departed from them without getting any nearer the truth. In such a case, he merely *means* to adopt the moral point of view, but has not succeeded. He has adopted something which he wrongly believes to be the moral point of view. He must still be called a person of good will because of his intentions, but he cannot arrive at true answers to his question. Clearly, our central problem is to define the moral point of view.

3 / Self-Interest and Morality

Throughout the history of philosophy, by far the most popular candidate for the position of the moral point of view has been self-interest. There are obvious parallels between these two standpoints. Both aim at the good. Both are rational. Both involve deliberation, the surveying and weighing of reasons. The adoption of either yields statements containing the word 'ought.' Both involve the notion of self-mastery and control over the desires. It is, moreover, plausible to hold that a person could not have a reason for doing anything whatsoever unless his behavior was designed to promote his own good. Hence, if morality is to have the support of reason, moral reasons must be self-interested, hence the point of view of morality and self-interest must be the same. On the other hand, it seems equally obvious that morality and self-interest are very frequently opposed. Morality often requires us to refrain from doing what self-interest recommends or to do what self-interest forbids. Hence it seems that morality and self-interest cannot be the same points of view.

Can we save the doctrine that the moral point of view is that of self-interest? One way of circumventing the difficulty just mentioned is to draw a distinction between two senses of 'self-interest,' shortsighted and enlightened. The shortsighted egoist always follows his short-range interest without taking into consideration how this will affect others and how their reactions will affect him. The enlightened egoist, on the other hand, knows that he cannot get the most out of life unless he pays attention to the needs of others on whose good will he depends. On this view, the standpoint of (immoral) egoism differs from that of morality in that it fails to consider the interests of others even when the long-range benefits to oneself are likely to be greater than the short-range sacrifices.

This view can be made more plausible still if we distinguish between those egoists who consider each course of action on its own merits and those who, for convenience, adopt certain rules of thumb which they have found will promote their long-range interest. Slogans such as 'Honesty is the best policy,' 'Give to charity rather than to the Department of Internal Revenue,' 'Always give a penny to a beggar when you are likely to be watched by your acquaintances,' 'Treat your servants kindly and they will work for you like slaves,' 'Never be arrogant to anyone—you may need his services one day,' are maxims of this sort. They embody the "wisdom" of a given society. The enlightened long-range egoist may adopt these as rules of thumb, that is, as *prima-facie* maxims, as rules which he will observe unless he has good evidence that departing from them will pay him better than abiding by them. It is obvious that the rules of behavior adopted by the enlightened egoist will be very similar to those of a man who rigidly follows our own moral code.

Moreover, this sort of egoism does not appear to be contrary to reason but, rather, to be required by it. For in the first place, the consistent enlightened egoist satisfies the categorical imperative, or at least one version of it, 'Act only on that maxim whereby thou canst at the same time will that it should become a universal law.' And in the second place, it seems to be superior to other forms of reasoning. For, as Sidgwick puts it, "I quite admit that when the painful necessity comes for another man to choose between his own happiness and the general happiness, he must as a reasonable being prefer his own, i.e. it is right for him to do this on my principle."[2]

Nevertheless it can be shown that this is not the point of view of morality. For those who adopt consistent egoism cannot make moral judgments. Moral talk is impossible for consistent egoists. But this amounts to a reductio ad absurdum of consistent egoism.

Let B and K be candidates for the presidency of a certain country and let it be granted that it is in the interest of either to be elected, but that only one can succeed. It would then be in the interest of B but against the interest of K if B were elected, and vice versa, and therefore in the interest of B but against the interest of K if K were liquidated, and vice versa. But from this it would follow that B ought to liquidate K, that it is wrong for B not to do so, that B has not "done his duty" until he has liquidated K; and vice versa. Similarly K, knowing that his own liquidation is in the interest of B and therefore anticipating B's attempts to secure it, ought to take steps to foil B's endeavors. It would be wrong for him not to do so. He would "not have done his duty" until he had made sure of stopping B. It follows that if K prevents B from liquidating him, his act must be said to be both wrong and not wrong—wrong because it is the prevention of what B ought to do, his duty, and wrong for B not to do it; not wrong because it is what K ought to do, his duty, and wrong for K not to do it. But one and the same act (logically) cannot be both morally wrong and not morally wrong. Hence in cases like these no moral judgments apply.

This is obviously absurd. For morality is designed to apply in just such cases, namely, those where interests

---

[2] Henry Sidgwick, *The Methods of Ethics*, 7th ed. (London: Macmillan and Co., 1907), pref. to the 6th ed., p. xvii.

conflict. But if the point of view of morality were that of self-interest, then there could *never* be moral solutions of conflicts of interest. However, when there are conflicts of interest, we always look for a "higher" point of view, one from which such conflicts can be settled. Consistent egoism makes everyone's private interest the "highest court of appeal." But by 'the moral point of view' we *mean* a point of view which furnishes a court of arbitration for conflicts of interest. Hence it cannot (logically) be identical with the point of view of the interest of any particular person or group of persons.

4 / Rules and Exceptions

A consistent egoist has only one supreme principle to which he does not make exceptions, namely, to do whatever is necessary for the promotion of his interest. All his other more specific maxims are merely rules of thumb designed to apply this principle to particular circumstances. If, in a particular case, they do not serve this end, then the consistent egoist would make an exception in his favor. A person who has adopted the moral point of view acts on a different supreme principle, namely, to do whatever is required by moral rules. All his other maxims are merely more specific rules of thumb designed to apply this principle to particular circumstances. The egoist's supreme principle requires him to make exceptions "in his favor," the moral person's supreme principle requires him not to make such exceptions.

Kant grasped this point even if only obscurely. He saw that adopting the moral point of view involves "acting on principle." It involves conforming to rules even when doing so is unpleasant, painful, costly, or ruinous to oneself. Kant, furthermore, argued that, since moral action is action on principle (and not merely in accordance with rules of thumb), moral rules are absolutely inflexible and without exceptions. Accordingly he concluded that if 'Thou shalt not kill' states a moral rule, then any and every act correctly describable as an act of killing someone must be said to be morally wrong.

Kant also saw that this view required him to reject some of our deepest moral convictions; we certainly think that the killing of a man in self-defense or by the hangman is not morally wrong. Kant was prepared to say that our moral convictions are wrong on this point. Can we salvage these moral convictions? The only alternative, to say that acting on principle does not require us not to make exceptions in our own favor, seems to be equally untenable.

It is therefore not surprising that many philosophers have abandoned Kant's (and the commonsense) view that the moral rightness of an act is its property of being in accordance with a moral rule or principle.

However, this whole problem arises only because of a misunderstanding of the expression 'making an exception in one's favor.' As soon as this is cleared up, it can be seen that Kant is right in saying that acting on principle implies making no exception in anyone's favor, but wrong in thinking that therefore all moral rules must be absolutely without exception.

'No parking in the city' has a number of recognized exceptions which are part of the rule itself, for example, 'except in the official parking areas,' 'except in front of a parking meter,' 'except on Saturday mornings and after 8 P.M. every day.' A person who does not know the recognized exceptions does not completely know the rule, for these exceptions more precisely delimit its range of application. A policeman who is not booking a motorist parking in front of a parking meter is not granting exemption to (making an exception in favor of) this motorist. On the contrary, he is administering the rule correctly. If he did apply the no-parking rule to the motorist, *he* would be applying it where *it* does not apply, because this is one of the recognized exceptions which are *part of* the rule. On the other hand, a policeman who does not book a motorist parking his vehicle in a prohibited area at peak hour on a busy day is making an exception in the motorist's favor. If he does so because the man is his friend, he illegitimately grants an exemption. If he does so because the motorist is a doctor who has been called to attend to a man lying unconscious on the pavement, this is a "deserving case" and he grants the exemption legitimately.

Apply this distinction to the rules of a given morality. Notice first that moral rules differ from laws and regulations in that they are not administered by special administrative organs such as policemen and magistrates. Everyone "administers" them himself. Nevertheless, it makes sense to speak of making exceptions in one's own favor. For one may refuse to apply the rule to oneself when one knows that it does apply, that is to say, one may refuse to observe it even when one knows one should. And what is true of making exceptions in one's own favor is true also of making them in favor of someone else. It is almost as immoral to make exceptions in favor of one's wife, son, or nephew as in favor of oneself.

When we say, therefore, that a person who has killed a burglar in self-defense has not done anything wrong, we are not making an exception in the houseowner's favor. It is much nearer the truth to say that, in our morality, the rule 'Thou shalt not kill' *has several recognized exceptions*, among them 'in self-defense.' We can say that a man does not know fully our moral

rule 'Thou shalt not kill' if he does not know that it
has, among others, this "exception," i.e., limit of application.

Like other rules of reason, our moral convictions
hold only *presumptively*.[3] Killing is wrong *unless* it is
killing in self-defense, killing by the hangman, killing
of an enemy in wartime, accidental killing, and possibly mercy killing. If it is one of these types of killing,
then it is *not* wrong.

Even if it is one of the wrongful acts of killing, it is
so only *prima facie*, other things being equal. For there
may have been an overriding moral reason in favor of
killing the man, for example, that he is about to blow
up a train and that this is the only way of stopping
him.

One further point should be made to avoid misunderstanding. Unlike laws and regulations, moral
rules have not been laid down by anyone. Knowing
moral rules cannot, therefore, involve knowing exactly
what a certain person has enjoined and forbidden and
what exceptions he has allowed, because there is no
such person. In the case of regulations and laws, it was
precisely this knowledge which enabled us to draw the
distinction between saying that someone was granting
an exception and saying that he was merely applying
the rule which, for cases of this sort, provided for an
exception. Our distinction seems to collapse for moral
rules.

However, the answer to this is simple. When a magistrate is empowered to make exceptions or grant exemptions in "deserving cases," the question of what is
a "deserving case" is not of course answered in the
regulation itself. If it were, the magistrate would not
be exercising his power to grant exemption, but would

[3] See above, Chapter One, section 4.

simply apply the regulation as provided in it. How, then, does the magistrate or policeman know what is a deserving case? The doctor who parks his car in a prohibited spot in order to attend to an injured man is such a case, namely, a *morally deserving* case. The principles in accordance with which policemen or magistrates grant exemptions to existing regulations are moral principles. In the case of moral rules, there cannot be any distinction between exceptions which are part of the rule and deserving cases. *Only* deserving cases can be part of the moral rule, and *every* deserving case is properly part of it. Hence while in the case of laws and regulations there is a reason for going beyond the exceptions allowed in the regulation itself (when there is a morally deserving instance), in the case of moral rules there is no such reason. For all deserving cases are, from the nature of the case, part of the moral rule itself. Hence it is never right to make an exception to a moral rule in anyone's favor. Kant is therefore quite right in saying that it is always wrong to make exceptions to moral rules in one's own favor (and for that matter in anyone else's), but he is wrong in thinking that this makes moral rules inflexible. For the fact that departing from it would be in the agent's interest is simply not a legitimate ground for making an exception to a moral rule, as it is for exceptions to a rule of self-interest.

5 / Moral Rules Are Meant for Everybody

The point of view of morality is inadequately characterized by saying that *I* have adopted it if *I* act on principles, that is, on rules to which I do not make exceptions whenever acting on them would frustrate one or the other of my purposes or desires. It is characterized by greater universality than that. It must be thought of as a standpoint from which rules are con-

sidered as being acted on *by everyone.* Moral rules
are not merely rules to which a person must not make
exceptions in his favor but they are principles *meant
for everybody.*

The teaching of morality must be completely universal and open. Morality is not the preserve of an
oppressed or privileged class or individual. People are
neglecting their duties if they do not teach the moral
rules to their children. Children are removed from the
homes of criminals because they are not likely to be
taught the moral rules there. An esoteric code, a set
of precepts known only to the initiated and perhaps
jealously concealed from outsiders, can at best be a
religion, not a morality. 'Thou shalt not eat beans and
this is a secret' or 'Always leave the third button of
your waistcoat undone, but don't tell anyone except
the initiated members' may be part of an esoteric
religion, but not of a morality. 'Thou shalt not kill, but
it is a strict secret' is absurd. 'Esoteric morality' is a
contradiction in terms. It is no accident that the so-
called higher religions were imbued with the missionary spirit, for they combine the beliefs of daemons
and gods and spirits characteristic of primitive religions with *a system of morality.* Primitive religions
are not usually concerned to proselytize. On the contrary, they are imbued with the spirit of the exclusive
trade secret. If one thinks of one's religion as concentrated wisdom of life revealed solely to the *chosen*
people, one will regard it as the exclusive property of
the club, to be confined to the elect. If, on the other
hand, the rules are thought to be for everyone to obey,
one must in consistency want to spread the message.

The condition of universal teachability yields three
other criteria of moral rules. They must not, in the
first place, be "self-frustrating." They are so if their
purpose is frustrated as soon as everybody acts on

them, if they have a point only when a good many people act on the opposite principle. Someone might, for instance, act on the maxim 'When you are in need, ask for help, but never help another man when he is in need.' If everybody adopted this principle, then their adoption of the second half would frustrate what obviously is the point of the adoption of the first half, namely, to get help when one is in need. Although such a principle is not self-contradictory—for anybody could consistently adopt it—it is nevertheless objectionable from the moral point of view, for it could not be taught openly to everyone. It would then lose its point. It is a parasitic principle, useful to anyone only if many people act on its opposite.

The same is true of "self-defeating" and "morally impossible" rules. A principle is self-defeating if its point is defeated as soon as a person lets it be known that he has adopted it, for example, the principle 'Give a promise even when you know or think that you can never keep it, or when you don't intend to keep it.' The very point of giving promises is to reassure and furnish a guarantee to the promisee. Hence any remark that throws doubt on the sincerity of the promiser will defeat the purpose of making a promise. And clearly to *let it be known* that one gives promises even when one knows or thinks one cannot, or when one does not intend to keep them, is to raise such doubts. And to say that one acts on the above principle is to imply that one may well give promises in these cases. Hence to reveal that one acts on this principle will tend to defeat one's own purpose.

It has already been said that moral rules must be capable of being taught openly, but this rule is self-defeating when taught openly, for then everyone would be known to act on it. Hence it cannot belong to the morality of any group.

Lastly, there are some rules which it is literally impossible to teach in the way the moral rules of a group must be capable of being taught, for example, the rule 'Always assert what you think not to be the case.' Such *morally impossible* rules differ from self-frustrating and self-defeating rules in that the latter could have been taught in this way, although it would have been quite senseless to do so, whereas the former literally cannot be so taught. The reason why the above rule cannot be taught in this way is that the only possible case of acting on it, doing so secretly, is ruled out by the conditions of *moral teaching*.

(1) Consider first someone secretly adopting this rule. His remarks will almost always mislead people, for *he will be taken to be saying what he thinks true,* whereas he *is* saying the opposite. Moreover, in most cases what he thinks (and not what he says) will be true. Thus, it will usually be the case that p is true when he says 'not-p,' and not-p when he says 'p,' whereas people will take it that p is true when he says 'p,' and not-p when he says 'not-p.' Thus communication between him and other people breaks down, since they will almost always be misled by him whether he wishes to mislead them or not. The possibility of communication depends on a speaker's ability *at will* to say either what he thinks to be the case or what he thinks not to be the case. Our speaker cannot communicate because by his principle he is forced to mislead his hearers.

Thus, anyone secretly adopting the principle 'Always assert what you think not to be the case' cannot communicate with others since he is bound to mislead them whether he wants to or not. Hence he cannot possibly teach the principle to anybody. And if he were to teach the principle without having adopted it himself, then, although he would be understood, those who adopted it would not. At any rate, since moral teaching involves teaching rules such as the taught may openly avow to be observing, this case is ruled out. A principle which is taught for secret acceptance only cannot be embodied in a *moral* rule of the group.

(2) Of course, people might soon come to realize what is the matter with our man. They may discover that in order not to be misled by what he says they have only to substitute '*p*' for 'not-*p*' and vice versa. But if they do this, then they have interpreted his way of speaking, not as a reversal of the general presumption that one says what one thinks is the case (and not the opposite), but as a change of the use of 'not.' In his language, it will be said, 'not' has become an affirmation sign, negation being effected by omitting it. Thus, if communication is to be possible, we must interpret as a change in usage what is intended as the reversal of the presumption that every assertion conveys what the assertor believes to be the case.

If everyone were, by accident, to adopt simultaneously and secretly our principle 'Always assert what you think is not the case,' then, for some time at least, communication would be impossible. If, on the other hand, it were adopted openly, then communication would be possible, but only if the adoption of this principle were to be accompanied by a change in the use of "not" which would completely cancel the effect of the adoption of the principle. In that case, however, it can hardly be said that the principle has been adopted.

(3) The case we are considering is neither (1) nor (2). We are considering the open teaching of the principle 'Alway assert what you think is not the case,' for open acceptance by everybody, an acceptance which is not to be interpreted as a change in the use of 'not.' But this is nonsense. We cannot all *openly* tell

one another that we are always going to mislead one another in a certain way and insist that we must continue to be misled, though we know how we could avoid being misled. I conclude that this principle could not be embodied in a rule belonging to the morality of any group.

These points are of general interest in that they clarify some valuable remarks contained in Kant's doctrine of the categorical imperative. In particular they clarify the expression "can will" contained in the formulation 'Act so that thou *canst will* thy maxim to become a universal law of nature.' "Canst will" in one sense means what I have called "morally possible." Your maxim must be a formula which is morally possible, that is, which is logically capable of being a rule belonging to the morality of some group, as the maxim "Always lie" is not. No one *can* wish that maxim to be a rule *of some morality*. To say that one is wishing it is to contradict oneself. One cannot wish it any more than one can wish that time should move backwards.

The second sense of "can will" is that in which no rational person can will certain things. Self-frustrating and self-defeating moral rules are not morally impossible, they are merely senseless. No rational person could wish such rules to become part of any morality. That is to say, anyone wishing that they should, would thereby expose himself to the charge of irrationality, like the person who wishes that he should never attain his ends or that he should (for no reason at all) be plagued by rheumatic pains throughout his life.

The points just made also show the weakness of Kant's doctrine. For while it is true that someone who acts on the maxim 'Always lie' acts on a morally impossible one, it is not true that every liar necessarily acts on that maxim. If he acts on a principle at all, it may, for instance, be 'Lie when it is the only way to avoid harming someone,' or 'Lie when it is helpful to you and harmful to no one else,' or 'Lie when it is entertaining and harmless.' Maxims such as these can, of course, be willed in either of the senses explained.

6 / Moral Rules Must Be for the Good of Everyone Alike

The conditions so far mentioned are merely formal. They exclude certain sorts of rule as not coming up to the formal requirements. But moral rules should also have a certain sort of content. Observation of these rules should be *for the good of everyone alike*. Thrasymachus' view that justice is the advantage of the stronger, if true of the societies of his day, is an indictment of their legal systems from the moral point of view. It shows that what goes by the name of morality in these societies is no more than a set of rules and laws which enrich the ruling class at the expense of the masses. But this is wrong because unjust, however much the rules satisfy the formal criteria. For given certain initial social conditions, formal equality before the law may favor certain groups and exploit others.

There is one obvious way in which something may be for the good of everyone alike, namely, if it furthers the common good. When I am promoted and my salary is raised, this is to my advantage. It will also be to the advantage of my wife and my family and possibly of a few other people—it will not be to the advantage of my colleague who had hoped for promotion but is now excluded. It may even be to his detriment if his reputation suffers as a result. If the coal miners obtain an increase in their wages, then this is to the advantage of coal miners. It is for their common good. But it may not be to the advantage of anyone else. On the other hand, if production is raised and with it everyone's living standard, that is literally to everyone's advantage. The rule 'Work harder,' if it has these consequences, is for the common good of all.

Very few rules, if any, will be for the common good of everyone. But a rule may be in the interest of everyone alike, even though the results of the observation of the rule are not for the common good in the sense explained. Rules such as 'Thou shalt not kill,' 'Thou shalt not be cruel,' 'Thou shalt not lie' are obviously, in some other sense, for the good of everyone alike. What is this sense? It becomes clear if we look at these rules from the moral point of view, that is, that of an independent, unbiased, impartial, objective, dispassionate, disinterested judge. Taking such a God's-eye point of view, we can see that it is in the interest of everyone alike that everyone should abide by the rule 'Thou shalt not kill.' From the moral point of view, it is clear that it is in the interest of everyone alike if everyone alike should be allowed to pursue his own interests provided this does not adversely affect someone else's interests. Killing someone in the pursuit of my interests would interfere with his.

There can be no doubt that such a God's-eye point of view is involved in the moral standpoint. The most elementary teaching is based on it. The negative version of the so-called Golden Rule sums it up: 'Don't do unto others as you would not have them do unto you.' When we teach children the moral point of view, we try to explain it to them by getting them to put themselves in another person's place: 'How would you like to have that done to you!' 'Don't do evil,' the most readily accepted moral rule of all, is simply the most general form of stating this prohibition. For doing evil is the opposite of doing good. Doing good is doing for another person what, if he were able to follow (self-interested) reason, he would do for himself. Doing evil is doing to another person what it would be contrary to reason for him to do to himself. Harming another, hurting another, doing to another what he dislikes having done to him are the specific forms this takes. Killing, cruelty, inflicting pain, maiming, torturing, deceiving, cheating, rape, adultery are instances of this sort of behavior. They all violate the condition of "reversibility," that is, that the behavior in question must be acceptable to a person whether he is at the "giving" or "receiving" end of it.

It is important to see just what is established by this condition of being for the good of everyone alike. In the first place, anyone who engages in nonreversible behavior is doing something wrong. It is irrelevant whether he knows that it is wrong or it, whether the morality of his group recognizes it or not. Such behavior is "wrong in itself," irrespective of individual or social recognition, irrespective of the consequences it has. Moreover, every single act of such behavior is wrong. We need not consider the whole group or the whole of humanity engaging in this sort of behavior, but only a single case. Hence we can say that all nonreversible behavior is morally wrong; hence that anyone engaging in it is doing what, prima facie, he ought not to do. We need not consider whether this sort of behavior has harmful consequences, whether it is forbidden by the morality of the man's group, or whether he himself thinks it wrong.

The principle of reversibility does not merely impose certain prohibitions on a moral agent, but also certain positive injunctions. It is, for instance, wrong—an omission—not to help another person when he is in need and when we are in a position to help him. The story of the Good Samaritan makes this point. The positive version of the Golden Rule makes the same point more generally: 'Do unto others as you would have them do unto you.' Note that it is wrong—not merely not meritorious—to omit to help others when they are in need and when you are in a position to help them. It does not follow from this, however, that it is wrong not to promote the greatest good of the greatest number, or not to promote the greatest amount of good in the world. Deontologists and utilitarians alike make the mistake of thinking that it is one, or the only one, of our moral duties to "do the optimific act." Nothing could be further from the truth. We do not have a duty to do good to others or to ourselves, or to others and/or to ourselves in a judicious mixture such that it produces the greatest possible amount of good in the world. We are morally required to do good only to those who are actually in need of our assistance. The view that we always ought to do the optimific act, or whenever we have no more stringent duty to perform, would have the absurd result that we are doing wrong whenever we are relaxing, since on those occasions there will always be opportunities to produce greater good than we can by relaxing. For the relief of suffering is always a greater good than mere enjoyment. Yet it is quite plain that the worker who, after a tiring day, puts on his slippers and listens to the radio is not doing anything he ought not to, is not neglecting any of his duties, even though it may be perfectly true that there are things he might do which produce more good in the world, even for himself, than merely relaxing by the fireside.

Chapter Six

THE SOCIAL FACTOR IN MORALITY

I now take for granted the following difference between moral reasoning and other forms of practical reasoning I have mentioned. I take it that the latter are simply various kinds of calculi whose use will enable an individual to act in such a way that he will thereby secure a greater amount of the good things in life and avoid more of the bad, than if he followed his natural inclinations. I take it that moral reasoning comes into the picture only when the goals of different individuals come into conflict with one another. For only then is there a need for reasons, generally regarded as superior to those already mentioned and designed, to adjudicate between the conflicting needs, wants, and aspirations of different individuals. I assume, then, that the existence of moral reasoning presupposes the normal interaction between persons. For a single man on a desert island, moral reasoning would be unnecessary and pointless, except on the assumption that he is in interaction with persons beyond his island, whether men or gods.

Our question now must be whether morality presupposes society as well as other individuals. Can there be a morality when individuals live in a state of nature, outside society? Is it not a fact, and is it not necessarily so, that morality comes into being only when men leave the state of nature and enter society? The question, in other words, appears to be whether morality is prior to society or comes afterwards, whether morality is the parent or the child of society. With this basic question a good many others are linked. Can people be moral by nature or must they be trained to be so by society? Are moral prohibitions dictated by human nature or do they arise out of the needs of society? Are our pangs of conscience and our guilt feelings the natural and untutored consequences of our doing wrong or are they the result of social conditioning? Are there eternal moral truths valid for all societies or are our moral convictions a matter of social convention? The answers to all these seem to follow from the answer to our basic question. But for this very reason, no answer to it is satisfactory.

As usual, a closer examination of the puzzle shows it to be a compound of several smaller questions. Our task is therefore more complex, but less perplexing than it appeared at first. Instead of having to unravel a seemingly insoluble big problem, we have to tackle a great many different small ones which are, severally, quite tractable. And since different answers are required for these minor questions, it is not surprising that no single answer to the major question which contains them all can be satisfactory.

In this chapter, I shall distinguish five minor questions which seem to me to be obscurely at the back of people's minds when they ask whether morality is prior or posterior to society: (a) whether or not there are some types of conduct which must be said to be right whatever changes occur in a given society: as there obviously are no types of conduct which must be said to be customary whatever the changes that occur in the society in question; (b) whether or not there are some types of conduct which must be said to be right even in the absence of any society whatsoever: as there obviously are no types of conduct which can be said to be customary in the absence of any society whatsoever; (c) whether, if there were such types of conduct, anyone could know, in the absence of any society whatsoever, that there were; (d) whether it is possible that people should, by nature, *be* moral or whether being moral involves having been trained to be; (e) whether social changes can have any influence on whether a certain type of conduct *is* right or merely on whether *it is believed* to be.

The answer to question (d) will enable us to determine the relative importance of human nature and society in man's morals, that is, in the extent to which men conform in their moral practice to what they believe and preach. The answers to questions (a), (c), and (d) will further clarify our understanding of how it is we know what is right and wrong. And the answer to question (b) will throw light on the conditions under which our system of moral concepts properly applies.

1 / True Moralities and Absolute Morality

Our discussion in the previous chapter has brought to light an essential characteristic of a morality: that it should make sense to ask, 'But are these moral convictions true?' or 'Is this moral code correct?' or words to that effect. The question implies that the moral rules and convictions of any group can and should be subjected to certain tests. It implies a distinction between this and that morality on the one hand and true morality on the other.

Let us be quite clear, however, what this distinction amounts to. It is not, in the first place, that between 'a morality' and 'morality as such,' which is analogous to the distinction between a legal system and law as such or between a disease and disease as such. Talking about a morality, say Greek or Tikopia or *fin de siècle* morality, is like talking about Roman, canonic, or Napoleonic law, or about Bright's disease, cancer, or leprosy. But talking about morality as such or the nature of morality is like talking about law as such or the nature of law, disease as such or the nature of disease. When talking in this way, we are drawing attention to the essentials of the concept. We are thinking of the conditions which something must satisfy in order to be properly called 'a morality,' 'a legal system,' 'a disease.' We are asked to neglect all those additional features in virtue of which a given morality, legal system, or disease is always more than just that, is always a particular one, Christian morality, or Napoleonic law, or hepatitis. Morality as such is not a supermorality, any more than law as such is a superlaw, or disease as such a superdisease. Morality as such is not even a morality, but a set of conditions. Morality as such cannot, therefore, be either true or false.

And this brings out an important point. There is no a priori reason to assume that there is only one true morality. There are many moralities, and of these a large number may happen to pass the test which moralities must pass in order to be called true. It would, therefore, be better to speak of 'a true morality' or of 'true moralities' than of 'true morality.'

However, there is one point that makes it desirable to speak of 'true morality' in addition to speaking of 'true moralities.' It is this. True moralities are particular moralities which pass certain tests. We may abstract from all the particular existential conditions of given moralities and think of true morality as a system of true moral convictions whose content is completely independent of the particular conditions of this or that way of life. There may therefore be true moral convictions which, though possibly no one actually holds them, are true in and for all possible social conditions. But there could be such true moral convictions only if their content had nothing to do with social conditions. It may, of course, be argued that there are no such convictions, but I think there are.

'True morality' in this sense cannot, of course, be just *one* moral code, the same for any morality which can be said to be true. For there will be many different moralities all of which are true, although each may contain moral convictions which would be out of place in one of the others. Thus, 'Lending money for interest is wrong,' 'A man ought not to marry his brother's widow,' 'It is wrong to take more than one wife,' and so on may be true moral convictions in one set of social conditions, but false in another. However, moral convictions, such as 'Killing is wrong,' 'Harming others is wrong,' 'Lying is wrong,' 'Misusing the institutions of one's society is wrong,' are true quite irrespective of the particular setup of given societies. If these are true moral convictions at all, then they must be absolutely true, for they are based solely on human nature. They are, from their very nature, independent of particular variations of the social pattern. However, they are not true for "all rational beings," as Kant thought, but only for human beings, and they would not necessarily remain true for human beings if there were radical changes in human nature. Thus, if being killed became generally desired and were a pleasurable experience and if one were reborn soon afterwards with a new body but with all memories intact, it would no longer be true that killing was wrong.

I shall, then, distinguish between true moralities and absolute morality. True moralities are actually embodied moralities, those forming part of a given way of life of a society or an individual, which would pass a certain test, if they were subjected to it. Absolute morality, on the other hand, is that set of moral convictions, whether held by anyone or not, which is true quite irrespective of any particular social conditions in which they might be embodied. Every true morality must contain as its core the convictions belonging to absolute morality, but it may also contain a lot more that could not be contained in every other true morality.

It is clear, furthermore, that true moralities are the applications of the most general true moral convictions to the specific conditions of a particular social order. 'It is wrong to misuse social institutions' is part of absolute morality, for it is neutral to the particular form the social institutions take. But even very general precepts, such as 'Stealing is wrong,' 'Adultery is wrong,' 'Promise breaking is wrong,' 'Neglecting your duties is wrong,' 'Failing to discharge your obligations is wrong,' cannot be part of absolute morality, for these refer to specific ways of misusing specific social institutions, which a given society may not have. It is conceivable that in a given society there might be no institution of property or marriage, no such thing as promising or having duties or obligations, and still the group might have a morality, for it might believe that killing is wrong or that hurting others is wrong.

2 / Absolute Moral Truths and the Existence of Society

There can be no reason to doubt, then, that there are moral truths unaffected by social changes. Does it follow from this fact that there would be moral truths even if there were no societies at all? Nothing can obviously be said to be customary or contrary to custom, legal or illegal, in the absence of any society whatsoever. Similarly, it might be argued, it would not make sense to say that something was right or wrong where people lived outside society. The question, then, is whether or not any types of conduct could be said to be morally right (or wrong) where people live "outside society," "in a state of nature." The moment the question is raised doubts about its meaningfulness arise. After all, "living in society" and "living outside society" are figurative expressions which we never actually employ. Do we know what we mean by them?

It must be admitted that these phrases sound odd, for we never have occasion to use them. As far as we can tell, people have always lived in societies. We can, however, imagine what it would be like for men to live "in a state of nature." If human beings lived in small, biologically necessary but relatively impermanent groups consisting of one man, one woman, and their dependent offspring, if they had no language or only the most rudimentary forms of one, if they had no fund of knowledge and practical skills to pass on, if they did not inculcate in their young certain uniform rules of behavior, then we would have to say that these people lived "outside" society. To live in a society is to live among men who have a common way of life which they pass on to their children. Societies are "artificial" ways of life, ways of life which go beyond the instinctive or natural and sometimes counter to it.

Our question, then, makes sense. We understand the difference between a state of affairs in which societies exist and one in which none exist. Our question now is whether anything could be said to be right (or wrong) in a state of nature, where no societies exist, as obviously nothing can be said to be legal and customary in such a state. One of the reasons why nothing can there be said to be legal or customary is inapplicable in the case of morality: it is self-contradictory to say, 'In a state of nature killing is illegal or contrary to custom,' but there is nothing self-contradictory in saying, 'In a state of nature it is wrong to kill.' For 'illegal' and 'contrary to custom' imply a reference to a given social system. 'Illegal' means 'illegal in x.' 'Contrary to custom' means 'contrary to custom in x.' There is no such thing as illegality or contrariness to custom apart from a society where it is so. 'Morally wrong' does not carry such implications, hence such remarks involve no self-contradiction.

But while not self-contradictory, claims of the form 'x is wrong in a state of nature' might nevertheless be necessarily false. The reason for this may not be that their contradictories are necessarily true, as in the case of 'Circles are not round,' or that they imply the nonexistence of one of the presuppositions of their being either true or false, as in 'Killing is illegal in the state of nature.' Such claims might be necessarily false because in a state of nature there is no rational justification for the very distinction between morally right and wrong. They might, in other words, be necessarily false because to say that there is a state of nature is to assert the absence of conditions whose presence constitutes the only justification for distinguishing between morally right and wrong. This is Hobbes's contention. In the state of nature, reason tells us that we would *all* do much better if we *all* followed certain rules, which he calls the laws of nature. At the same time, reason also tells us not to obey these laws in that state because we have reason to think that other people will not follow them and we would do better not to follow them than to be the only ones to do so. Thus, Hobbes's account of the state of nature amounts to the claim that in such a state every statement is necessarily false which claims that some course of action is morally wrong. For to say that something is morally wrong is to imply that one ought not to do it, that to refrain from doing it is in accordance with reason. But it is Hobbes's main contention that in the state of nature to refrain from doing what is "wrong," that is, what is prohibited by the law of nature, is not in accordance with reason.

Is Hobbes's argument sound? What are its steps? The premise is that, in the absence of restrictions imposed by law, men will act either on impulse or in accordance with self-interest. From this Hobbes deduces that there will be perpetual conflict between men. For above everything else, men want to live. Because of the scarcity of resources, one man's luxury means another man's poverty. It is therefore in everyone's interest to secure for himself as great a share of them as possible, to hoard them for future emergencies, to defend them against all possible attacks, to engage in preventive action against others who might become a menace, and so on. In the absence of laws and agencies of law enforcement, there is therefore, and in reason ought to be, a perpetual war of everyone against everyone. As is well known, Hobbes thought that there was only one way out: the formation, by contract among all individuals, of an absolute ruler, a Leviathan, to whom every single man hands over all his rights and powers and who, in return, lays down and rigidly enforces laws. When this Sovereign is established, everybody knows that anyone transgressing the law will be punished. Each individual therefore has reason to obey the law and each, moreover, knows that all the others have reason to obey it, too. Everyone, therefore, has reason to expect that everyone else will obey it.

It has often been pointed out that this argument, as it stands, is unsound. For in a state of nature, the formation of a contract could not have had the desired effect. Between people who act only on impulse or in accordance with self-interest, mutual trust cannot be created by any sort of undertaking. Nor can a Leviathan be created by it. The state cannot come into being when no one can rely on anyone else to act in accordance with the rules, but only on impulse or as it serves his interest. No power could be concentrated in the hands of one person by the device of all others "handing over" their power to him, for power cannot be handed over by words alone. Otherwise the power of the Secretary General of the United Nations would be quite adequate.

However, Hobbes's point can be made in a way not open to this objection. True, a state of mutual trust cannot be brought about, in a state of nature, by the conclusion of a contract, but adequate mutual trust prevails in most societies, whether legal or prelegal, simply because there are established ways of behavior. Some societies do not have even a primitive legal system, but merely a set of customs which establish uniform ways of behavior and sufficient trust between its members. For every member knows that almost every other member will invariably behave in accordance with custom and not always on impulse or as his advantage dictates. Hobbes is merely wrong in thinking that a legal system can come into being by the conclusion of a mutual contract and that only a legal system can provide conditions of mutual trust. Hobbes may be quite right in his main point: only the existence of societies, that is, artificial, common, generally acknowledged, and generally followed ways of life can satisfy all the conditions for the application of moral concepts. Only when there are societies is it correct to say of any line of action that it is morally right or wrong, that one ought to do what is right and refrain from doing what is wrong, and that one ought to satisfy all the other demands of morality.

The question whether Hobbes is right on this point or not cannot be answered in this chapter, but will have to be postponed until Chapter Seven, section 3.

3 / Is Knowledge of Right and Wrong Possible in a State of Nature?

Even if Hobbes's argument is rejected that, outside society, nothing can *be* right or wrong, it might still be maintained that in such a state nothing could *be known* to be so. The most obvious reason for saying this is that, as has been shown, our knowledge of right and wrong depends on our ability to work out in deliberation what is so. Doing so in turn presupposes our ability to survey the facts with a view to determining which of them are moral pros and cons and our ability to weigh them against each other in order to ascertain which are the weightiest reasons. But is it not obvious that this ability requires training, that it presupposes a level of sophistication of which an individual cannot be capable unless he has been helped by the experience of generations? In conditions in which individuals have no cultural heritage to pass on to their children, no common skills, no common knowledge, no common rules of behavior, where language is at best quite primitive, there surely can be no system of reasoning at all, let alone one sufficiently elaborate to allow for specifically moral deliberations.

As already mentioned, the most popular answer to this would be the theory that our knowledge of right and wrong is not a matter of calculation relying on premises which require the experience of countless generations, but a sort of "seeing" or "intuiting" like knowing that something is yellow or that it is soft. Just as we know "immediately" or "intuitively" what is yellow by our eyes and what is soft by our fingers, so we know what is right and what is wrong by our conscience or moral sense. There is no need to worry about the way we learn the words 'right' and 'wrong.' We can discriminate colors before we learn the color words. If we did not, we could never learn them. Similarly, we can discriminate between right and wrong before we learn the words for these properties. Otherwise, how could we ever pick up what these words meant?

Dismissing the obvious objection that there is no such moral sense or inner eye, could we not say that our moral sense was a supersenory sense, a sense which did not depend on a sense organ, or perhaps depended on one which we had not yet discovered? We could know whether a man was musical or unmusical even if he had no ears, or artistic even if he had no eyes. All that is necessary is that he should appreciate the right sorts of result. In any case, why postulate a special moral sense, it might be asked. We have one already: reason. Reason is a faculty like sight. As sight enables us to see what color or shape an object has, so reason enables us to see whether an action is right or wrong. We need not be concerned about the objection that if reason were a faculty like sight then there would have to be a corresponding sensory organ. For in the first place there is such an organ: the brain. Cut out the brain or certain portions of it, and you destroy a person's ability to reason, just as you destroy his sight if you cut out his eyes. In the second place, sight is something over and above eyes. Some people have eyes and yet they are blind. Sight works in and through the organ of sight. Similarly reason is something over and above the brain, though it works in and through this organ.

If we accepted this analogy, then an immoral person would merely be like someone who surrounds himself with bad pictures because he lacks artistic discrimination. If the difference between right and wrong were known "naturally" by a moral sense, whether sensory or supersensory, then we would always have to excuse an immoral person, provided only his moral convictions differed from ours or provided he claimed that he had no moral sense, no ability to discriminate between right and wrong, and therefore no moral convictions. We would have to excuse him as we excuse a tone-deaf or a color-blind man for not being able to appreciate music or painting. Some admirers of certain artists have indeed wished to excuse their callous behavior toward their wives and friends by describing them not as immoral but as "amoral," which they construe on the model of unmusicality.

A person who has an artistic sense but nevertheless surrounds himself with trash is simply foolish or perverse. He is like one who, not liking spinach, eats it regularly and for no reason at all. Clever crooks are not foolish or perverse. For despite the Film Production Code crime often pays, and pays handsomely, provided the criminals are clever and ruthless. I am tone deaf and therefore to be pitied. I am deprived of one of the greatest and most deeply satisfying experiences, I am told. I am excluded from a certain sort of refined delight. Crooks are not deprived of any specific experiences, or refined delights. Their self-centeredness and insensitivity to the needs and wishes of others, their callous egoism and brutality are not due to their lack of a specific sense which makes it impossible for them to "see" or "hear" or "savor" or "intuit" the difference between right and wrong.

Therefore, remarks to the effect that reason enables us to "see" what is right and what is wrong can be and have been seriously misleading, for they naturally suggest that reason is a faculty like sight affording us special sensations or nonsensory sensations, sometimes called "intuitions" or "insights" (such as that certain conclusions are false or that killing is wrong), which enable us to perform the activities of reason. In fact, it is the other way round. 'Reason' is the name of the power to perform the activities of reason, which are of the general nature of calculations, the results of which are propositions such as that a certain conclusion is false or a certain act morally wrong. (I have given an account of some of the activities of so-called practical reason in Chapters One and Two and throughout the book.) It would therefore be better to say that reason is the power *to work out,* rather than the power to "see," the answers to certain questions.

It is now clear that we could not tell, in the state of nature, what is in accordance with or contrary to reason, what we ought or ought not to do, or what is morally right and what morally wrong. For if reason is not the power to "see" this, but the power to work it out in deliberation, then we must have the highly sophisticated skill of deliberating. But it has already been demonstrated that it is practically impossible for a person living outside society to acquire this skill.

4 / Being Moral By Nature

I will now take it for granted that there is no such thing as moral intuition or seeing by reason what is right and wrong. Nevertheless it may be held that we are so equipped by nature as to be able, without having to think, to do what is right and to shun what is wrong. It may not be necessary for us to do anything but to follow nature, impulse, or instinct in order to do right and avoid doing wrong. Nature or God might have implanted in us the promptings of conscience prior to acting and the pangs of conscience and the feelings of guilt when we have disregarded the warnings. In that case we would still know by nature and in a state of nature what is right and wrong. Training in a society would not be necessary. Of course, it would then be a mistake to say that we did certain things because we discovered we ought to do them and refrained from doing others because we found out they were wrong. We would have to say, rather, that we knew that certain things were right and others wrong because our conscience *prompted us* in certain ways, that is, because we were naturally driven to do or to shun certain things.

Can being moral consist simply in following nature? What in any case is meant by 'following nature'? Suppose someone follows his reason—is he following nature or is he not? It is, of course, natural to follow reason and unnatural, perverse, to do what one knows is contrary to reason. On the other hand, in following reason one is not following nature, as one is when following impulse, inclination, or instinct. Following the latter is doing what comes naturally, what one would do naturally, that is, without thinking or deliberating. On the other hand, one cannot follow reason without thinking or deliberating. There is nothing perverse in following reason: it is natural in this sense. But there is nothing spontaneous, unconsidered, unthought-out about following reason: it is not natural in that sense.

In what sense, then, is it maintained that being moral is following nature? It is not claimed in this context that being moral is not perverse, unnatural, against nature, but that being moral is uncritically following the promptings of human nature, without first examining and weighing these promptings, possibly following and possibly resisting them.

We can dismiss without much empirical investigation the theory that all men are always by nature moral. It is a plain fact that many people often are inclined to do what they think or know is wrong and not to do what they think or know they ought to do. This plain fact of our experience is compatible with the present theory only on the basis of a further assumption which is also quite obviously false: the assumption that these immoral inclinations or promptings are *always* due to social influences and never to innate tendencies. Anyone who has ever dealt with children knows how untrue this assumption is.

The alternative to this is no more plausible. It consists in saying that human beings have both moral and nonmoral impulses which may conflict. I mention only one objection to this view: we could never know which were the moral ones and which the others. For how could we distinguish between moral, immoral, and nonmoral promptings if we had only the promptings to go by? These promptings do not come from different places. And even if they did, why should we take any notice of that? Why should we never follow promptings coming from one place and always only those coming from another? Why should we assume that there are promptings with a good origin or status and others with a bad one? How would we distinguish 'higher' from 'lower' promptings if we had only origins to go by?

If it is admitted that we are not always prompted by nature to do what is right and to shun what is wrong, then it must be admitted also that this cannot be the way we know what is right and wrong. In any case, how could we know whether nature *always* prompted us to do what is right and to shun what is wrong unless we already knew, *independently*, what was right and what wrong?

Even if it were true and we could somehow know

that we always naturally did what was right and shunned what was wrong, even then the present view would not be tenable. For being moral cannot consist in following nature. If it did consist in this, then animals or robots could be moral, provided only they had the correct natural endowment. In the case of such creatures all the praise and blame must go to the person who has endowed them. We do not praise or blame a digital computer. It acts the way it does because it has been "programed" in this way. If being moral consisted in following nature, our maker would deserve all the credit *and all the blame.* There could not be, in the case of such creatures, any question of resisting or yielding to temptation, of being conscientious or negligent, of making an effort or of being lax. Such people would always, automatically, blindly, and without thinking or trying, do what is right and shun what is wrong.

However, such creatures are not moral beings, and only moral beings can be moral. They are not moral beings because they are incapable of acting contrary to their inclinations or promptings. A moral being must be able to keep his natural impulses in check, to control himself, to do what is required by the weightiest moral reasons, even if this means thwarting the strongest present inclination.

The point is that no creature could be so equipped with natural inclinations that he is guaranteed to do in all possible situations what is required by morality. Killing, stealing, hurting, lying, are indeed wrong, other things being equal. But whether a particular course of action is right or wrong, all things considered, depends on the circumstances in which the person finds himself. It is indeed fortunate that most people have a horror of killing and hurting others, a natural inclination to be kind and to help others in need, for in ordinary circumstances morality will require just these types of action. Quite often, however, the morally required thing will be to kill someone, to hurt someone, or to tell lies. We must attack, perhaps wound and kill, the man who attacks our wife and children or an enemy soldier in wartime. We must not be kind and helpful to a drunkard resisting arrest however much our heart beats for him. The moral man cannot rely on any innate tendency, for he may be in circumstances in which he ought to resist rather than follow it. Everybody must be prepared for this. Of course, those who are badly endowed by nature, such as the homicidally inclined person, must make a particularly great effort and must make it often. But the "well-endowed" person is also sometimes required to make it. He who cannot hurt a fly must overcome his natural tendencies almost as often as the homicidal type his. For societies are often involved in wars, and even in peace we must often refuse, reject, or thwart the demands of others, in the service of justice, in doing our duty, or in keeping our promises. A kindly Vice-Chancellor who cannot say 'No' to anybody is almost as bad as a tough one who says 'No' to everybody. If we were not capable of resisting our kindly tendencies, we would often be unable to satisfy the demands of morality.

5 / What Society Adds To Absolute Morality

That the existence of societies is a good thing is beyond all reasonable doubt. Human beings "outside" society can live only the most primitive animallike lives. They have no chance of achieving a full or satisfying life. Without education, without language, without a cultural heritage to draw on, without the division of labor, without skills, without an ordered and settled way of life, existence is a continuous struggle against nature, leaving no time for any of the things that are most worth while.

Not the least important contribution which the existence of a society makes to the life that is worth living is the provision of established patterns of behavior giving everyone confidence and security. It provides institutions and definite rules for the realization of the most fundamental human needs and desires. It makes arrangements about mating and the rearing of children, about the ways individual members of the society may use their talents to earn a living, and the like. Such arrangements give rise to specific injunctions and prohibitions which will be common knowledge among the members of the group. In view of the great advantages of established ways of behavior, such rules and institutions usually have the backing of the morality of the group. Rules such as 'Thou shalt not steal,' 'Thou shalt not commit adultery,' 'Honour thy father and thy mother,' 'Help the members of your family' are general, society-neutral rules giving moral backing to whatever specific arrangements a given society might make about sex, property, and the family.

Social institutions of this sort introduce a great many differentiations between people. They create social positions and social status, attaching special privileges and duties, thus modifying the otherwise uniform picture of moral relations between members of the group. In addition to the rules arising out of the institutions of the society, there are the special rights and duties arising out of the various patterns of life which a society allows. In order that the various problems confronting each man should be more efficiently met, society arranges for a division of labor, allotting different tasks to different groups and making arrangements guaranteeing that a sufficient number of people is allocated to each task. In some societies, some are born to rule, others to be soldiers, others merchants, craftsmen, or manufacturers, others to till the land, and yet others to be untouchables performing the most menial tasks. In other societies, each individual is free to choose whatever path of life he wishes, free perhaps to change from one pattern to another if he can do so and if he so desires.

Apart from those fixed patterns of life which give rise to special obligations and rights there is in some societies, including our own, an arrangement whereby any individual can enter into special moral ties with other members by voluntary acts, such as promises or contracts.

5.1   UPSETTING AND RESTORING THE MORAL EQUILIBRIUM

So far, we have considered only primary moral rules, that is, those which prohibit or enjoin certain types of behavior, such as 'Thou shalt not kill,' 'Thou shalt not steal,' 'Thou shalt help thy neighbour when he is in need of your help,' and so on. Secondary rules of morality are those which prohibit or enjoin certain types of behavior *in response to* some "upset of the moral balance," for example, 'An eye for an eye, a tooth for a tooth,' 'Let him who is free from guilt throw the first stone,' 'One good turn deserves another.'

What is it to "upset the moral balance"? The moral balance is preserved when everyone is "strictly minding his own business." Plato was right in connecting morality with minding one's own business; he was wrong only in his explanation of the connection. Minding one's own business and not interfering with anyone else are not all there is to morality, though it is true that when everyone minds his own business the moral equilibrium is maintained. This equilibrium can be upset in two quite different ways. I may behave in a manner which upsets the moral balance against me or in my favor. I may accumulate a moral debit or credit account; the first when I do what I ought not to do, the second when I do "more than my duty"; the first when I violate a "rule of duty," the second when I observe a "rule of supererogation." When, for example, I kill someone, steal something, am cruel to someone, or commit adultery, I am accumulating a moral debit balance. If, on the other hand, at great risk to myself I save someone's life or make great financial sacrifices for the sake of a good cause, I am acquiring a moral credit balance. It is for cases of this sort that the secondary moral rules are devised. Primary moral rules define what it is, morally speaking, to mind one's own business, to preserve the moral equilibrium. Secondary moral rules indicate what is to be done by whom when the balance has been upset.

Secondary moral rules are determined by the concept of desert, of positive or negative moral merit. They state what a person deserves, that is, ought to get or have done to him, as a result of the upset of the moral balance. A person who has not upset the moral balance deserves nothing. He has neither positive nor negative moral merit.

The aim of a morality is to prevent the upsetting of the moral equilibrium by violation of "rules of duty" and to encourage it by the observation of "rules of supererogation." At the same time, the methods of deterring and encouraging potential rule breakers must not themselves interfere with the primary rules. The secondary rules are therefore seen as designed to "restore the moral balance." They have the object of deterring or encouraging rule breakers, but also of bringing the process to an end. When the balance is "restored," the secondary rules no longer apply.

Take first the case of preventing violations of rules of duty. An obvious, if crude, way of "restoring the moral equilibrium" is provided by the institution of revenge. The person injured returns the harm. The supreme principle governing such secondary rules is 'One bad turn deserves another.' This has the serious disadvantage that it is difficult to "restore" the moral equilibrium. Since revenge is itself the infliction of harm on an individual, the secondary rule applies again. In the institution of the vendetta or the blood feud, what is designed to discourage violations of primary moral rules in fact leads to endless mutual harming.

The substitution of punishment for revenge remedies this drawback. The infliction of hardship on the wrong-doer is taken out of the hands of the injured person or his aggrieved relations and handed over to a disinterested official. By making a ceremony of it, it is clearly indicated that this is not intended as merely the infliction of harm on an individual, but as the application of a secondary moral rule designed to "restore" the moral balance. The object of the practice is to deter future wrongdoers. The infliction of hardship on a given individual is justified by his prior violation of a primary moral rule. There is now no aggrieved person left. Punishment has restored the moral equilibrium. The wrongdoer has expiated, atoned for, his wrong. Everyone has a clean slate again. It is wrong for the aggrieved to continue to harbor a grudge, to refuse to forgive the wrongdoer.

The situation is somewhat different in the case of an upset of the moral balance by observing (not breaking) a rule of supererogation. Obviously, the point of these rules is that they should be observed rather than broken, although observing them (not breaking them) constitutes an upset of the moral equilibrium. Such breaches of the moral equilibrium are desirable. In order to encourage them, we have secondary rules of morality, guided by the general principle 'One good

turn deserves another.' We say that a person who
engages in works of supererogation thereby acquires
moral desert or merit.

5.2 UNIVERSALIZABILITY

Lastly, society has to prohibit those courses of action
which, because of the particular nature of the social
framework, would be harmful if everyone or even if
only a few people entered on them. Because of social
interaction not foreseeable by ordinary members of the
society, some people may suffer harm as the result of
a single individual's conduct or as the result of a large
number engaging in that sort of conduct. The society
is then entitled to prohibit such conduct. No harm is
done if one person walks across the lawn. But the
lawn is ruined if everyone does. No harm is done if
one person uses the gas. But if everyone uses it during
peak hours, then the gas supply may break down, and
everyone will be adversely affected.

Is such behavior morally objectionable? We seem to
imply that it is, by the well-known formula 'You can't
do that; what if everyone did the same!' Kant thought
of it as the essence of his categorical imperative, 'Act
only on that maxim whereby thou canst at the same
time will that it should become a universal law.' This
is precisely what we "cannot will" in the cases in question. Although it is not true that, as Kant put it, a will
willing such a maxim to become a universal law would,
literally, contradict itself, nevertheless, in making such
a maxim *a universal law,* one would enjoin people to
do evil, and such a law would obviously be wrong.

It is, however, important to distinguish behavior
which is thus "nonuniversalizable" from behavior that
is "nonreversible," as we called it. The latter can be
seen to be *wrong in itself,* irrespective of the consequences and of how many people engage in it. This is

not so in the case of nonuniversalizable behavior. There we have to consider the consequences, and not merely of a single act but of a great many of them. There is nothing wrong in itself with putting one straw on the camel's back, but one of them will be the last.

What exactly does this prove? That no one is allowed to lay even one straw on the camel's back? That every act of this kind is wrong? Surely not. Before we can say that any act of this sort is wrong, a number of conditions must be satisfied.

In the first place, all concerned must be *equally entitled* to behave in the nonuniversalizable way. It would, for instance, be most undesirable if everyone had dinner at 6:30 P.M., for all the nation's service would then come to a standstill at that time. But it cannot follow from this that eating at 6:30 P.M. is wrong for everyone. It cannot follow because the argument applies equally for any time, and it must be all right to eat at *some* time. Of course, there is no serious problem here. Not everyone is equally entitled to have his dinner at 6:30 P.M. Those who are on duty at that time must have it before or after or while they are attending to their duties.

There are further conditions. If everyone were to be celibate henceforth, mankind would die out, and even prior to extinction, the reduction in number would make life unbearable. Those who do not find the prospect of the end of the human race upsetting will have to admit that the return to primitive conditions is undesirable. Again, if everyone suddenly stopped smoking, drinking, gambling, and going to the pictures, some states might go bankrupt and this would be undesirable. All the same, it can hardly be true that abstinence in matters of sex, smoking, drinking, gambling, and visits to the cinema can be wrong in any and every case, even though we are surely all equally entitled to refrain from these ways of spending our time.

There must, therefore, be a further condition. Everyone must not only be equally entitled to engage in these forms of activity, but people must also be inclined to do so. There would have to be a real danger that, unless they are stopped somehow, many will engage in this sort of behavior. People are lazy, so they will not go to the polling booth or make the detour round the newly planted lawn. People like picking flowers, so they will destroy the rare wild flowers. People want to heat their rooms, so they will want to use their radiators during peak hours. But there is no great danger that they will all go celibate, or give up smoking and drinking.

This point, by the way, shows that nonuniversalizability cannot be adduced to show that suicide is wrong. Suicide is no more wrong than celibacy and for the same reason. People are less keen on suicide even than on celibacy. There is no danger of the race dying out. In fact, all over the world people are so keen on procreation that the suicide rate could go up a long way before anyone need be alarmed. Of course if, one day, life and sex were to become burdens to all of us and if, nevertheless, it really is desirable that the race should go on, then reckless suicide or slothful celibacy might become morally wrongful types of conduct. Until then, those weary of life and sex need not have a bad conscience about their uncommon indulgences.

There is one further point in this. To say that it is wrong to walk across the lawn or switch on the gas during peak hours, provided (a) it would have undesirable consequences *if* everyone did it, (b) we are all equally entitled to do it, and (c) doing it is an indulgence, not a sacrifice, amounts to saying that since refraining from doing these things is a sacrifice such a sacrifice for the common good should not be demanded of one or a few only, but equally of all, even if a universal sacrifice is not needed. Since no one is more entitled than anyone else to indulge himself and since *all* cannot do so without the undesirable consequences which no one wants, *no one* should be allowed to indulge himself.

Now the conditions are complete. If the behavior in question is such that (i) the consequences would be undesirable if everyone did it, (ii) all are equally entitled to engage in it, and (iii) engaging in this sort of behavior is an indulgence, not a sacrifice, then such behavior *should be prohibited by the morality of the group*.

But now suppose that it is not prohibited. Is it wrong all the same? Kant certainly thought so. I think he is mistaken. For since, by indulging in the behavior in question, I am not actually doing any harm, my behavior is not wrong in itself, but only when taken in conjunction with that of others. I cannot prevent the evil by refraining. Others must refrain too. In the case of nonreversible behavior, *my action alone* is the cause of the evil. I can avoid the evil if I refrain. In the case under discussion, however, if I have reason to suppose that the others will not refrain, I surely have reason not to refrain either, as the only reason for refraining is to avert the evil consequences. If these cannot be avoided, there is no reason why I should make a sacrifice. If the grass is not going to grow anyway, why should I make the detour?

It is no good arguing that I am not entitled to do wrong just because other people might or probably would. For I am not doing wrong. I have no moral reason for the sacrifice. I need no justification or excuse, for my behavior is wrong only *if I have no ade-*

quate reason to think that others will refuse to make the sacrifice. If I have adequate reason to think they will refuse to make it, then I have adequate reason to think that my own sacrifice will be in vain; hence I have adequate reason against making it.

Of course, if the results are *very* undesirable and my sacrifice is *very* small and I am not very certain what the others will do, I should take the risk of making the sacrifice even if it turns out to have been in vain. But, otherwise, reason will support the opposite course.

The situation is different if the morality or the custom or the law of the group does already contain a rule forbidding such behavior. If there is such a rule, then the behavior is wrong, for such a rule has the backing of morality. As we have said, a group ought to have rules forbidding nonuniversalizable behavior. And when there is such a rule, then the community has regulated behavior of this sort and I ought to do my share toward the success of the regulation.

I should like to add one word about the morality of individual initiative in these matters. Some people think that individuals should go ahead with a good example and not wait until the rule-making powers of the group are used. Others argue that this is putting too great a burden on the public-spirited. Thus, compulsory military service with exemptions granted to those engaged in important national industries is said by some to be fairer, volunteering for national service is said by others to be morally preferable. I can see no reason for the latter view. It may indeed seem preferable from the military point of view, for it may be argued that volunteers are better soldiers. But there is no reason why if keenness is wanted volunteers should not have preferential rights to serve in the army rather than in industry. On the other hand, there is no reason why the sacrifices involved in the defense of their country should be borne only by those who are taking their moral responsibilities seriously, and no reason why those who are not should benefit gratuitously. In the absence of argument showing that the method of individual initiative yields a more efficient army, the other seems to me preferable and, in any case, obviously fairer. Hesitation to use the lawmaking force of the community is understandable, for such use may endanger individual freedom, but often this hesitation is supported on the grounds of the moral preferability of individual sacrifice and initiative. Such arguments seem to me unsound.

Ideally, then, any given morality would be the application of absolute morality to the special social conditions of the group in question. With regard to any actual way of life, we must therefore ask not only whether it incorporates the rules of absolute morality, but also whether these general rules have been properly applied to the specific social conditions or whether there are any arrangements which are open to criticism from the moral point of view. It is obvious that in hardly any society will the work of applying the principles of absolute morality to individual social conditions have been performed flawlessly. The temptations to which ruling classes are exposed, for example, to impose laws which will be to their own economic advantage, have frequently been noticed. So has the temptation to pass off these self-interested laws as the proper rules of morality. Thrasymachus and Marx are inclined to say that actual moralities are no more than the selfish rules laid down by the ruling class. This is not likely to be true, but even if it were, it would show no more than that actually existing moralities contain a high proportion of, or only, false moral convictions. It does not show that such perversions of morality are all there is to morality.

Chapter Seven

WHY SHOULD WE
BE MORAL?

We are now in a position to deal with the various problems we shelved earlier. In Chapter Two we had to postpone the examination of how we verify those fundamental propositions which serve as major premises in our practical arguments. We must now deal with this. The examination of the prevailing consideration-making beliefs used at the first stage of our practical deliberations leads naturally to the examination of our rules of superiority used at the second stage. This in turn involves our investigating whether moral reasons are superior to all others and whether and why we should be moral. That opens up the most fundamental issue of all, whether and why we should follow reason.

1 / The Truth of Consideration-Making Beliefs

Let us begin with our most elementary consideration-making belief: the fact that if I did x I would enjoy doing x is a reason for me to do x. There can be little doubt that this is one of the rules of reason recognized in our society. Most people would use the knowledge of the fact that they would enjoy doing something as a pro in their deliberations whether to do it. When we wonder whether to go to the pictures or to a dinner dance, the fact that we would enjoy the dinner dance but not the pictures is regarded as a reason for going to the dinner dance rather than to the pictures. We are now asking whether this widely held belief is correct or true, whether this fact really is a reason or is merely and falsely believed to be so.

What exactly are we asking? Is our question empirical? Obviously it cannot be answered by direct inspection. We cannot see, hear, or smell whether this belief is true, whether this fact is a reason or not. The nature of our question becomes clearer if we remind ourselves of the function of consideration-making beliefs, namely, to serve as major premises in practical arguments. These arguments are supposed to yield true answers to questions of the form 'What shall I do?' or 'What is the best course of action open to me?' The matter is considerably simplified by the fact that, at this point, we are dealing merely with prima-facie reasons. In order to determine the truth of the premise, we have only to find out whether the conclusion based on it is the best, *other things being equal,* that is, whether it is better than the conclusions based on its contradictory or its contrary.

The problem of the truth or falsity of consideration-making beliefs is thus reduced to the question whether it is better that they, rather than their contraries or contradictories, should be used as rules of reason, that is, as major premises in practical arguments. How would we tell?

Our practical argument runs as follows:

(i) The fact that if I did *x* I would enjoy doing *x* is a reason for me to do *x*.

(ii) I would enjoy doing x if I did x.

(iii) Therefore I ought to do x (other things being equal).

It is not difficult to see that the contrary of our rule of reason is greatly inferior to it. For if, instead of the presently accepted belief (see above (i)), its contrary became the prevailing rule, then anyone trying to follow reason would have to conclude that whenever there is something that he would enjoy doing if he did it then he ought *not* to do it. "Reason" would counsel everyone always to refrain from doing what he enjoys, from satisfying his desires. "Reason" would counsel self-frustration for its own sake.

It is important to note that such an arrangement is possible. To say that we would not now *call* it 'following reason' is not enough to refute it. We can imagine two societies in which English is spoken and which differ only in this, that in one society (i) is accepted, in the other the contrary of (i). It would then be correct to say in one society that doing what one would enjoy doing was following reason, in the other society that it was acting contrary to it. The "tautologousness" of the first remark *in our society* is not incompatible with the "tautologousness" of the contrary remark *in another society*. From the fact that the proposition 'Fathers are male' is analytic, we can infer that 'fathers are male' is necessarily true. But this is so only because we would not correctly *call* anything 'father' that we would correctly call 'not male.' And it is perfectly in order to say that in any society in which English was spoken but in which the words 'father' and/or 'male' were not used in this way those words did not mean quite the same as in our society. And with this, the matter is ended, for we are not concerned to settle the question which verbal arrangement, ours or theirs, is the better. Nothing of importance follows from the fact that a society has our usage of 'father' and 'male' or theirs. But in the case of the use of 'reason,' much depends on which usage is accepted. The real difficulty only begins when we have concluded, correctly, that the word 'reason' is used in a different sense in that other society. For the practical implications of the word 'reason' are the same in both societies, namely, that people are encouraged to follow reason rather than to act contrary to it. However, *what* is held in one society to be in accordance with reason is held to be contrary to it in the other. Hence, we must say that in practical matters nothing fundamental can be settled by attention to linguistic proprieties or improprieties.

What, then, is relevant? We must remember what sort of a "game" the game of reasoning is. We ask the question 'What shall I do?' or 'What is the best course of action?' Following reasons is following those hints which are most likely to make the course of action the best in the circumstances. The criteria of 'best course of action' are linked with what we mean by 'the good life.' In evaluating a life, one of the criteria of merit which we use is how much satisfaction and how little frustration there is in that life. Our very purpose in "playing the reasoning game" is to maximize satisfactions and minimize frustrations. Deliberately and for no further reason to frustrate ourselves and to minimize satisfaction would certainly be to go counter to the very purpose for which we deliberate and weigh the pros and cons. These criteria are, therefore, necessarily linked with the very purpose of the activity of reasoning. Insofar as we enter on that "game" at all, we are therefore bound to accept these criteria. Hence we are bound to agree that the consideration-making belief which is prevalent in our society is better than its contrary.

But need we accept that purpose? Is this not just a matter of taste or preference? Could not people with other tastes choose the opposite purpose, namely, self-frustration and self-denial rather than satisfaction of desires and enjoyment? The answer is No, it is not just a matter of taste or preference. Whether we like or don't like oysters, even whether we prefer red ink to claret, is a matter of taste, though to prefer red ink is to exhibit a very eccentric taste. Whether we prefer to satisfy our desires or to frustrate them is not, however, a matter of taste or preference. It is not an eccentricity of taste to prefer whatever one does *not* enjoy doing to whatever one does enjoy doing. It is perverse or crazy if it is done every now and then, mad if it is done always or on principle.

It might be objected that these people would merely be *called* mad by us—this does not prove that they really are, any more than the fact that they might well call us mad proves that we are. This objection seems to take the sting out of the epithet 'mad.' However, it only seems to do so, because it is misconstrued on one of the following two models.

(i) 'They are called artesian wells, but that's only what we call them in this country.' In this case, the distinction is between what we all, quite universally but incorrectly, call them in this country and what they really are, that is, what they are properly and correctly called. The difference is between an established but incorrect usage, and the correct but possibly not established usage. However, people who prefer whatever they do not enjoy doing to whatever they do would not merely generally (though incorrectly) but quite correctly be called mad.

(ii) 'When two people quarrel and call each other "bastard," that does not prove that they are bastards.' On this model, it might be argued that the word 'mad' has no established usage, that we use it only in order to insult people who are not average. But this is untenable. Admittedly we often use the word 'mad' to insult people who are not mad, just as we use the word 'bastard' to insult people who were born in wedlock. But we could not use these words for these purposes unless they were correctly used to designate characteristics generally regarded as highly undesirable. When a person is certified insane, this is done not just because he differs from average, but because he is different in certain fundamental and undesirable respects. To prove the undesirability of these differences, it is enough here to point out that no one *wants* to become mad. Our conclusion must be that there is a correct use of the word 'mad' and that people who prefer whatever they do not enjoy doing to whatever they do enjoy doing differ from normal people in just such fundamental and undesirable respects as would make the word 'mad' correctly applicable to them.

The contradictory of our most fundamental consideration-making belief is also less satisfactory than *it* is. If it were to be believed that the fact that one would enjoy doing *x* was not a reason for doing it (a belief which is the contradictory of our most fundamental consideration-making belief), then people wishing to follow reason would be neither advised to do what they would enjoy doing nor advised not to do it. Reason would simply be silent on this issue. Never to do what one would enjoy doing would be as much in accordance with reason (other things being equal) as always to do it. In such a world, "following reason" might in the long run be less rewarding than following instinct or inclination. Hence this cannot *be* following reason, for in the long run it *must* pay to follow reason at least as much as to follow instinct or inclination, or else it is not reason.

To sum up. People who replace our most fundamental consideration-making belief by its contrary or contradictory will not do as well as those who adhere to it. Those who adopt its contrary must even be said to be mad. This seems to me the best possible argument for the preferability of our fundamental consideration-making belief to its contrary and contradictory. And this amounts to a proof of its correctness or truth. I lack space to examine whether the other consideration-making beliefs prevalent in our society are also true. Perhaps enough has been said to enable readers to conduct this investigation for themselves.

2 / The Hierarchy of Reasons

How can we establish rules of superiority? It is a prima-facie reason for me to do something not only that *I* would enjoy it if *I* did it, but also that *you* would enjoy it if *I* did it. People generally would fare better if this fact were treated as a pro, for if this reason were followed, it would create additional enjoyment all round. But which of the two prima-facie reasons is superior when they conflict? How would we tell?

At first sight it would seem that these reasons are equally good, that there is nothing to choose between them, that no case can be made out for saying that people generally would fare better if the one or the other were treated as superior. But this is a mistake.

Suppose I could be spending half an hour in writing a letter to Aunt Agatha who would enjoy receiving one though I would not enjoy writing it, or alternatively in listening to a lecture which I would enjoy doing. Let us also assume that I cannot do both, that I neither enjoy writing the letter nor dislike it, that Aunt Agatha enjoys receiving the letter as much as I enjoy listening to the lecture, and that there are no extraneous considerations such as that I deserve es pecially to enjoy myself there and then, or that Aunt Agatha does, or that she has special claims on me, or that I have special responsibilities or obligations to please her.

In order to see which is the better of these two reasons, we must draw a distinction between two different cases: the case in which someone derives pleasure from giving pleasure to others and the case where he does not. Everyone is so related to certain other persons that he derives greater pleasure from doing something together with them than doing it alone because in doing so he is giving them pleasure. He derives pleasure not merely from the game of tennis he is playing but from the fact that in playing he is pleasing his partner. We all enjoy pleasing those we love. Many of us enjoy pleasing even strangers. Some even enjoy pleasing their enemies. Others get very little enjoyment from pleasing anybody.

We must therefore distinguish between people with two kinds of natural make-up: on the one hand, those who need not always choose between pleasing themselves and pleasing others, who can please themselves *by* pleasing others, who can please themselves more by not merely pleasing themselves, and, on the other hand, those who always or often have to choose between pleasing themselves and pleasing others, who derive no pleasure from pleasing others, who do not please themselves more by pleasing not merely themselves.

If I belong to the first kind, then I shall derive pleasure from pleasing Aunt Agatha. Although writing her a letter is not enjoyable in itself, as listening to the lecture is, I nevertheless derive enjoyment from writing it because it is a way of pleasing her and I enjoy pleasing people. In choosing between writing the letter and listening to the lecture, I do not therefore have to choose between pleasing her and pleasing myself. I have merely to choose between two different ways of pleasing myself. If I am a man of the second kind, then I must choose between pleasing myself and pleasing her. When we have eliminated all possible moral reasons, such as standing in a special relationship to the person, then it would be strange for someone to prefer pleasing someone else to pleasing himself. How strange this is can be seen if we substitute for Aunt Agatha a complete stranger.

I conclude from this that the fact that I would enjoy it if *I* did x is a better reason for doing x than the fact that you would enjoy it if *I* did x. Similarly in the fact that I would enjoy doing x if I did it I have a reason for doing x which is better than the reason for doing y which I have in the fact that you would enjoy doing y as much as I would enjoy doing x. More generally speaking, we can say that self-regarding reasons are better than other-regarding ones. Rationally speaking, the old quip is true that everyone is his own nearest neighbor.

This is more obvious still when we consider the case of self-interest. Both the fact that doing x would be in my interest and the fact that it would be in someone else's interest are excellent prima-facie reasons for me to do x. But the self-interested reason is better than the altruistic one. Of course, interests need not conflict, and then I need not choose. I can do what is in both our interests. But sometimes interests conflict, and then it is in accordance with reason (prima facie) to prefer my own interest to someone else's. That my making an appplication for a job is in *my* interest is a reason for me to apply, which is better than the reason against applying, which I have in the fact that my not applying is in *your* interest.

There is no doubt that this conviction is correct for all cases. It is obviously better that everyone should look after his own interest than that everyone should neglect it in favor of someone else's. For whose interest should have precedence? It must be remembered that we are considering a case in which there are no special reasons for preferring a particular person's interests to one's own, as when there are no special moral obligations or emotional ties. Surely, in the absence of any *special* reasons for preferring someone else's interests, *everyone's* interests are best served if *everyone* puts his own interests first. For, by and large, everyone is himself the best judge of what is in his own best interest, since everyone usually knows best what his plans, aims, ambitions, or aspirations are. Moreover, everyone is more diligent in the promotion of his own interests than that of others. Enlightened egoism is a possible, rational, orderly system of running things, enlightened altruism is not. Everyone can look after himself, no one can look after everyone else. Even if everyone had to look after only two others, he could not do it as well as looking after himself alone. And if he has to look after only one person, there is no advantage in making that person some one other than himself. On the contrary, he is less likely to know as well what that person's interest is or to be as zealous in its promotion as in that of his own interest.

For this reason, it has often been thought that enlightened egoism is a possible rational way of running things. Sidgwick, for instance, says that the principle of egoism, to have as one's ultimate aim one's own greatest happiness, and the principle of universal benevolence, to have as one's ultimate aim the greatest happiness of the greatest number, are equally rational.[1] Sidgwick then goes on to say that these two principles may conflict and anyone who admits the rationality of

[1] Henry Sidgwick, *The Methods of Ethics,* 7th ed. (London: Macmillan and Co., 1907), concluding chapter, par. 1.

both may go on to maintain that it is rational not to abandon the aim of one's own greatest happiness. On his view, there is a fundamental and ultimate contradiction in our apparent intuitions of what is reasonable in conduct. He argues that this can be removed only by the assumption that the individual's greatest happiness and the greatest happiness of the greatest number are both achieved by the rewarding and punishing activity of a perfect being whose sanctions would suffice to make it always everyone's interest to promote universal happiness to the best of his knowledge.

The difficulty which Sidgwick here finds is due to the fact that he regards reasons of self-interest as being no stronger and no weaker than moral reasons. This, however, is not in accordance with our ordinary convictions. It is generally believed that when reasons of self-interest conflict with moral reasons, then moral reasons override those of self-interest. It is our common conviction that moral reasons are superior to all others. Sidgwick has simply overlooked that although it is prima facie in accordance with reason to follow reasons of self-interest and also to follow moral reasons nevertheless, when there is a conflict between these two types of reason, when we have a self-interested reason for doing something and a moral reason against doing it, there need not be an ultimate and fundamental contradiction in what it is in accordance with reason to do. For one type of reason may be *stronger* or *better* than another so that, when two reasons of different types are in conflict, it is in accordance with reason to follow the stronger, contrary to reason to follow the weaker.

3 / The Supremacy of Moral Reasons

Are moral reasons really superior to reasons of self-interest as we all believe? Do we really have reason on our side when we follow moral reasons against self-interest? What reasons could there be for being moral? Can we really give an answer to 'Why should we be moral?' It is obvious that all these questions come to the same thing. When we ask, 'Should we be moral?' or 'Why should we be moral?' or 'Are moral reasons superior to all others?' we ask to be given a reason for regarding moral reasons as superior to all others. What is this reason?

Let us begin with a state of affairs in which reasons of self-interest are supreme. In such a state everyone keeps his impulses and inclinations in check when and only when they would lead him into behavior detrimental to his own interest. Everyone who follows reason will discipline himself to rise early, to do his exercises, to refrain from excessive drinking and smoking, to keep good company, to marry the right sort of girl, to work and study hard in order to get on, and so on. However, it will often happen that people's interests conflict. In such a case, they will have to resort to ruses or force to get their own way. As this becomes known, men will become suspicious, for they will regard one another as scheming competitors for the good things in life. The universal supremacy of the rules of self-interest must lead to what Hobbes called the state of nature. At the same time, it will be clear to everyone that universal obedience to certain rules overriding self-interest would produce a state of affairs which serves everyone's interest much better than his unaided pursuit of it in a state where everyone does the same. Moral rules are universal rules designed to override those of self-interest when following the latter is harmful to others. 'Thou shalt not kill,' 'Thou shalt not lie,' 'Thou shalt not steal' are rules which forbid the inflicting of harm on someone else even when this might be in one's interest.

The very *raison d'être* of a morality is to yield reasons which overrule the reasons of self-interest in those cases when everyone's following self-interest would be harmful to everyone. Hence moral reasons are superior to all others.

"But what does this mean?" it might be objected. "If it merely means that we do so regard them, then you are of course right, but your contention is useless, a mere point of usage. And how could it mean any more? If it means that we not only do so regard them, but *ought* so to regard them, then there must be *reasons* for saying this. But there could not be any reasons for it. If you offer reasons of self-interest, you are arguing in a circle. Moreover, it cannot be true that it is always in my interest to treat moral reasons as superior to reasons of self-interest. If it were, self-interest and morality could never conflict, but they notoriously do. It is equally circular to argue that there are moral reasons for saying that one ought to treat moral reasons as superior to reasons of self-interest. And what other reasons are there?"

The answer is that we are now looking at the world from the point of view of *anyone*. We are not examining particular alternative courses of action before this or that person; we are examining two alternative worlds, one in which moral reasons are always treated by everyone as superior to reasons of self-interest and one in which the reverse is the practice. And we can see that the first world is the better world, because we can see that the second world would be the sort which Hobbes describes as the state of nature.

This shows that I ought to be moral, for when I ask the question 'What ought I to do?' I am asking, 'Which is the course of action supported by the best reasons?' But since it has just been shown that moral reasons are superior to reasons of self-interest, I have been given a reason for being moral, for following moral reasons rather than any other, namely, they are better reasons than any other.

But is this always so? Do we have a reason for being moral whatever the conditions we find ourselves in? Could there not be situations in which it is not true that we have reasons for being moral, that, on the contrary, we have reasons for ignoring the demands of morality? Is not Hobbes right in saying that in a state of nature the laws of nature, that is, the rules of morality, bind only *in foro interno?*

Hobbes argues as follows.

(i) To live in a state of nature is to live outside society. It is to live in conditions in which there are no common ways of life and, therefore, no reliable expectations about other people's behavior other than that they will follow their inclination or their interest.

(ii) In such a state reason will be the enemy of co-operation and mutual trust. For it is too risky to hope that other people will refrain from protecting their own interests by the preventive elimination of probable or even possible dangers to them. Hence reason will counsel everyone to avoid these risks by preventive action. But this leads to war.

(iii) It is obvious that everyone's following self-interest leads to a state of affairs which is desirable from no one's point of view. It is, on the contrary, desirable that everybody should follow rules overriding self-interest whenever that is to the detriment of others. In other words, it is desirable to bring about a state of affairs in which all obey the rules of morality.

(iv) However, Hobbes claims that in the state of nature it helps nobody if a single person or a small group of persons begins to follow the rules of morality, for this could only lead to the extinction of such individuals or groups. In such a state, it is therefore contrary to reason to be moral.

(v) The situation can change, reason can support morality, only when the presumption about other people's behavior is reversed. Hobbes thought that this could be achieved only by the creation of an absolute ruler with absolute power to enforce his laws. We have already seen that this is not true and that it can also be achieved if people live in a society, that is, if they have common ways of life, which are taught to all members and somehow enforced by the group. Its members have reason to expect their fellows generally to obey its rules, that is, its religion, morality, customs, and law, even when doing so is not, on certain occasions, in their interest. Hence they too have reason to follow these rules.

Is this argument sound? One might, of course, object to step (i) on the grounds that this is an empirical proposition for which there is little or no evidence. For how can we know whether it is true that people in a state of nature would follow only their inclinations or, at best, reasons of self-interest, when nobody now lives in that state or has ever lived in it?

However, there is some empirical evidence to support this claim. For in the family of nations, individual states are placed very much like individual persons in a state of nature. The doctrine of the sovereignty of nations and the absence of an effective international law and police force are a guarantee that nations live in a state of nature, without commonly accepted rules that are somehow enforced. Hence it must be granted that living in a state of nature leads to living in a state in which individuals act either on impulse or as they think their interest dictates. For states pay only lip service to morality. They attack their hated neighbors when the opportunity arises. They start preventive wars in order to destroy the enemy before he can deliver his knockout blow. Where interests conflict, the stronger party usually has his way, whether his claims are justified or not. And where the relative strength of the parties is not obvious, they usually resort to arms in order to determine "whose side God is on." Treaties are frequently concluded but, morally speaking, they are not worth the paper they are written on. Nor do the partners regard them as contracts binding in the ordinary way, but rather as public expressions of the belief of the governments concerned that for the time being their alliance is in the interest of the allies. It is well understood that such treaties may be canceled before they reach their predetermined end or simply broken when it suits one partner. In international affairs, there are very few examples of *Nibelungentreue,* although statesmen whose countries have kept their treaties in the hope of profiting from them usually make such high moral claims.

It is, moreover, difficult to justify morality in international affairs. For suppose a highly moral statesman were to demand that his country adhere to a treaty obligation even though this meant its ruin or possibly its extinction. Suppose he were to say that treaty obligations are sacred and must be kept whatever the consequences. How could he defend such a policy? Perhaps one might argue that someone has to make a start in order to create mutual confidence in international affairs. Or one might say that setting a good example is the best way of inducing others to follow suit. But such a defense would hardly be sound. The less skeptical one is about the genuineness of the cases in which nations have adhered to their treaties from a sense of moral obligation, the more skeptical one must be about the effectiveness of such examples of virtue in effecting a change of international practice. Power politics still govern in international affairs.

We must, therefore, grant Hobbes the first step in his argument and admit that in a state of nature people, as a matter of psychological fact, would not follow the dictates of morality. But we might object to the next step that knowing this psychological fact about other people's behavior constitutes a reason for behaving in the same way. Would it not still be immoral for anyone to ignore the demands of morality even though he knows that others are likely or certain to do so, too? Can we offer as a justification for morality the fact that no one is entitled to do wrong just because someone else is doing wrong? This argument begs the question whether it *is* wrong for anyone in this state to disregard the demands of morality. It cannot be wrong to break a treaty or make preventive war if we have no reason to obey the moral rules. For to say that it is wrong to do so is to say that we ought not to do so. But if we have no reason for obeying the moral rule, then we have no reason overruling self-interest, hence no reason for keeping the treaty when keeping it is not in our interest, hence it is not true that we have a reason for keeping it, hence not true that we ought to keep it, hence not true that it is wrong not to keep it.

I conclude that Hobbes's argument is sound. Moralities are systems of principles whose acceptance by everyone as overruling the dictates of self-interest is in the interest of everyone alike, though following the rules of a morality is not of course identical with following self-interest. If it were, there could be no conflict between a morality and self-interest and no point in having moral rules overriding self-interest. Hobbes is also right in saying that the application of this system of rules is in accordance with reason only under social conditions, that is, when there are well-established ways of behavior.

The answer to our question 'Why should we be moral?' is therefore as follows. We should be moral because being moral is following rules designed to overrule reasons of self-interest whenever it is in the interest of everyone alike that such rules should be generally followed. This will be the case when the needs and wants and aspirations of individual agents conflict with one another and when, in the absence of such overriding rules, the pursuit of their ends by all concerned would lead to the attempt to eliminate those who are in the way. Since such rules will always require one of the rivals to abandon his pursuit in favor of the other, they will tend to be broken. Since, ex hypothesi it is in everyone's interest that they should be followed, it will be in everyone's interest that they should not only be taught as "superior to" other reasons but also adequately enforced, in order to reduce the temptation to break them. A person instructed in these rules can acknowledge that such reasons are superior to reasons of self-interest without having to admit that he is always or indeed ever attracted or moved by them.

But is it not self-contradictory to say that it is in a person's interest to do what is contrary to his interest? It certainly would be if the two expressions were used in exactly the same way. But they are not. We have already seen that an enlightened egoist can acknowledge that a certain course of action is in his enlightened long-term, but contrary to his narrow short-term interest. He can infer that it is "in his interest" and according to reason to follow enlightened long-term interest, and "against his interest" and contrary to reason to follow short-term interest. Clearly, "in his interest" and "against his interest" here are used in

new ways. For suppose it is discovered that the probable long-range consequences and psychological effects
on others do not work out as predicted. Even so we
need not admit that, in this new and extended sense,
the line of action followed merely seemed but really
was not in his interest. For we are now considering
not merely a single action but a policy.

All the same, we must not make too much of this
analogy. There is an all-important difference between
the two cases. The calculations of the enlightened egoist properly allow for "exceptions in the agent's favor."
After all, his calculus is designed to promote his interest. If he has information to show that in his particular circumstances it would pay to depart from a
well-established general canon of enlightened self-
interest, then it is proper for him to depart from it. It
would not be a sign of the enlightened self-interest of
a building contractor, let us say, if he made sacrifices
for certain subcontractors even though he knew that
they would or could not reciprocate, as subcontractors
normally do. By contrast, such information is simply
irrelevant in cases where moral reasons apply. Moral
rules are not designed to serve the agent's interest
directly. Hence it would be quite inappropriate for
him to break them whenever he discovers that they
do not serve his interest. They are designed to adjudicate primarily in cases where there is a conflict of interests so that from their very nature they are bound
to be contrary to the interest of one of the persons
affected. However, they are also bound to serve the
interest of the other person, hence his interest in the
other's observing them. It is on the assumption of
the likelihood of a reversal of roles that the universal
observation of the rule will serve everyone's interest.
The principle of justice and other principles which we
employ in improving the moral rules of a given society

help to bring existing moralities closer to the ideal which is in the interest of everyone alike. Thus, just as following the canons of enlightened self-interest is in one's interest only if the assumptions underlying it are correct, so following the rules of morality is in everyone's interest only if the assumptions underlying it are correct, that is, if the moral rules come close to being true and are generally observed. Even then, to say that following them is in the interest of everyone alike means only that it is better for everyone that there should be a morality generally observed than that the principle of self-interest should be acknowledged as supreme. It does not of course mean that a person will not do better for himself by following self-interest than by doing what is morally right, when others are doing what is right. But of course such a person cannot *claim* that he is following a superior reason.

It must be added to this, however, that such a system of rules has the support of reason only where people live in societies, that is, in conditions in which there are established common ways of behavior. Outside society, people have no reason for following such rules, that is, for being moral. In other words, outside society, the very distinction between right and wrong vanishes.

4 / Why Should We Follow Reason?

But someone might now ask whether and why he should follow reason itself. He may admit that moral reasons are superior to all others, but doubt whether he ought to follow reason. He may claim that this will have to be proved first, for if it is not true that he ought to follow reason, then it is not true that he ought to follow the strongest reason either.

What is it to follow reason? It involves two tasks, the theoretical, finding out what it would be in accordance with reason to do in a certain situation, what contrary to reason, and the practical task, to act accordingly. It was shown in Chapter Two how this is done. We must also remind ourselves that there are many different ways in which what we do or believe or feel can be contrary to reason. It may be *irrational,* as when, for no reason at all, we set our hand on fire or cut off our toes one by one, or when, in the face of conclusive evidence to the contrary, someone *believes* that her son killed in the war is still alive, or when someone is *seized by fear* as a gun is pointed at him although he knows for certain that it is not loaded. What we do, believe, or feel is called irrational if it is the case not only that there are conclusive or overwhelming reasons against doing, believing, or feeling these things, but also that we must know there are such reasons and we still persist in our action, belief, or feeling.

Or it may be *unreasonable,* as when we make demands which are excessive or refuse without reason to comply with requests which are reasonable. We say of demands or requests that they are excessive if, though we are entitled to make them, the party against whom we make them has good reasons for not complying, as when the landlord demands the immediate vacation of the premises in the face of well-supported pleas of hardship by the tenant.

Being unreasonable is a much weaker form of going counter to reason than being irrational. The former applies in cases where there is a conflict of reasons and where one party does not acknowledge the obvious force of the case of the other or, while acknowledging it, will not modify his behavior accordingly. A person is irrational only if he flies in the face of reason, if, that is, all reasons are on one side and he acts contrary to it when he either acknowledges that this is so or, while refusing to acknowledge it, has no excuse for failing to do so.

Again, someone may be *inconsistent,* as when he refuses a Jew admission to a club although he has always professed strong positive views on racial equality. Behavior or remarks are inconsistent if the agent or author professes principles adherence to which would require him to say or do the opposite of what he says or does.

Or a person may be *illogical,* as when he does something which, as anyone can see, cannot or is not at all likely to lead to success. Thus when I cannot find my glasses or my fountain pen, the logical thing to do is to look for them where I can remember I had them last or where I usually have them. It would be illogical of me to look under the bed or in the oven unless I have special reason to think they might be there. To say of a person that he is a logical type is to say that he always does what, on reflection, anyone would agree is most likely to lead to success. Scatterbrains, people who act rashly, without thinking, are the opposite of logical.

When we speak of following reason, we usually mean 'doing what is supported by the best reasons because it is so supported' or perhaps 'doing what we think (rightly or wrongly) is supported by the best reasons because we think it is so supported.' It might, then, occur to someone to ask, 'Why should I follow reason?' During the last hundred years or so, reason has had a very bad press. Many thinkers have sneered at it and have recommended other guides, such as the instincts, the unconscious, the voice of the blood, inspiration, charisma, and the like. They have advocated that one should not follow reason but be guided by these other forces.

However, in the most obvious sense of the question 'Should I follow reason?' this is a tautological question like 'Is a circle a circle?'; hence the advice 'You should not follow reason' is as nonsensical as the claim 'A circle is not a circle.' Hence the question 'Why should I follow reason?' is as silly as 'Why is a circle a circle?' We need not, therefore, take much notice of the advocates of unreason. They show by their advocacy that they are not too clear on what they are talking about.

How is it that 'Should I follow reason?' is a tautological question like 'Is a circle a circle?' Questions of the form 'Shall I do this?' or 'Should I do this?' or 'Ought I to do this?' are, as was shown (in Chapter Two), requests to someone (possibly oneself) to deliberate on one's behalf. That is to say, they are requests to survey the facts and weigh the reasons for and against this course of action. These questions could therefore be paraphrased as follows. 'I wish to do what is supported by the best reasons. Tell me whether this is so supported.' As already mentioned, 'following reason' means 'doing what is supported by the best reasons.' Hence the question 'Shall (should, ought) I follow reason?' must be paraphrased as 'I wish to do what is supported by the best reasons. Tell me whether doing what is supported by the best reasons is doing what is supported by the best reasons.' It is, therefore, not worth asking.

The question 'Why should I follow reason?' simply does not make sense. Asking it shows complete lack of understanding of the meaning of 'why questions.' 'Why should I do this?' is a request to be given the reason for saying that I should do this. It is normally asked when someone has already said, 'You should do this' and answered by giving the reason. But since 'Should I follow reason?' means 'Tell me whether doing what is supported by the best reasons is doing what is supported by the best reasons,' there is simply no possibility of adding 'Why?' For the question now comes to this, 'Tell me the reason why doing what is supported by the best reasons is doing what is supported by the best reasons.' It is exactly like asking, 'Why is a circle a circle?'

However, it must be admitted that there is another possible interpretation to our question according to which it makes sense and can even be answered. 'Why should I follow reason?' may not be a request for a reason in support of a tautological remark, but a request for a reason why one should enter on the theoretical task of deliberation. As already explained, following reason involves the completion of two tasks, the theoretical and the practical. The point of the theoretical is to give guidance in the practical task. We perform the theoretical only because we wish to complete the practical task in accordance with the outcome of the theoretical. On our first interpretation, 'Should I follow reason?' meant 'Is the practical task completed when it is completed in accordance with the outcome of the theoretical task?' And the answer to this is obviously 'Yes,' for that is what we mean by 'completion of the practical task.' On our second interpretation, 'Should I follow reason?' is not a question about the practical but about the theoretical task. It is not a question about whether, given that one is prepared to perform both these tasks, they are properly completed in the way indicated. It is a question about whether one should enter on the whole performance at all, whether the "game" is worth playing. And this is a meaningful question. It might be better to "follow inspiration" than to "follow reason," in this sense: better to close one's eyes and wait for an answer to flash across the mind.

But while, so interpreted, 'Should I follow reason?'

makes sense, it seems to me obvious that the answer to it is 'Yes, because it pays.' Deliberation is the only reliable method. Even if there were other reliable methods, we could only tell whether they were reliable by checking them against this method. Suppose some charismatic leader counsels, 'Don't follow reason, follow me. My leadership is better than that of reason'; we would still have to check his claim against the ordinary methods of reason. We would have to ascertain whether in following his advice we were doing the best thing. And this we can do only by examining whether he has advised us to do what is supported by the best reasons. His claim to be better than reason can in turn only be supported by the fact that he tells us precisely the same as reason does.

Is there any sense, then, in his claim that his guidance is preferable to that of reason? There may be, for working out what is supported by the best reasons takes a long time. Frequently, the best thing to do is to do something quickly now rather than the most appropriate thing later. A leader may have the ability to "see," to "intuit," what is the best thing to do more quickly than it is possible to work this out by the laborious methods of deliberation. In evaluating the qualities of leadership of such a person, we are evaluating *his ability to perform correctly the practical task of following reason* without having to go through the lengthy operations of the theoretical. Reason is required to tell us whether anyone has qualities of leadership better than ordinary, in the same way that pencil and paper multiplications are required to tell us whether a mathematical prodigy is genuine or a fraud.

Lastly, it must be said that sometimes it may be better even for an ordinary person without charisma not to follow reason but to do something at once, for quick action may be needed.

Index